What they are saying about *Elders at the Gate*

So much of history, so much of the story of American Christianity, is one generation's diagnosis of and attempted correction to the mistakes of their parent's generation, and how those corrections often result in new faults for the next generation to abhor and reject. This generational resentment has caused much pain, but it takes significant wisdom and perspective to overcome its temptations. My friend, Ray Blunt, offers here an exploration of how we might restore generational bonds so that young and old might learn together and enrich one another. As someone who has pursued faithfulness with his life, Ray shares lessons and stories that will help us do the same so that we might better love God and perhaps share lessons of our own as *Elders at the Gate* in our time.

        Michael Wear—Author of *Reclaiming Hope: Lessons Learned in the Obama White House About the Future of Faith in America* and Chief Strategist for The AND Campaign, a movement to advance redemptive justice in America.

I have known Ray Blunt for over 55 years. He has always run the race hard and now, playing in the fourth quarter, he is dedicated to finishing strong and poring his wisdom into younger lives that are on the field for their first kick off. If you are an "elder" and you wish to enhance those players coming behind, you need to be at the stadium "gate." Ray's book, *Elders at the Gate,* is the play book you need to finish strong and bring wisdom and life lessons to those who are playing in their first quarter.

        Bruce Fister—Lt. General (retired), Air Force Special Operations Commander and Executive Director of Officers Christian Fellowship and author of *Growing and Building: Faith, Prayer, and Leadership.*

Long known as a master teacher, Ray Blunt has been drawn in by governments, businesses and schools to make sure that true learning takes place—at the heart of his vision has been a commitment to the meaning of mentoring. Simply said, we learn the things that matter most in apprenticeship, over-the-shoulder and through-the-heart. We must see that words can become flesh to believe them to be true. In his new book, *Elders at the Gate*, Blunt brings together years of his life, inviting all of us into the world of his own work, teaching the next generation. His words deserve a very wide reading—among parents and educators, pastors and professionals—because his book is very good, a gift to everyone everywhere from a master of mentoring.

Steven Garber—Author of *Visions of Vocation*, and Professor of Marketplace Theology & Director of the Program in Leadership, Theology and Society, Regent College, Vancouver, BC.

ELDERS AT THE GATE

Kay — You have been living this story for some time. Thank you for sharing the wisdom of experience. May we all persist until we are home.

God's grace —
Ray

ELDERS
AT THE
GATE

A CALL TO REPAIR THE GENERATIONAL LINKS

RAY BLUNT

WordCrafts

The elders no longer sit in the city gates;
the young no longer dance and sing.

Lamentations 5:14

CONTENTS

Dedication

For my wife, B.J. Ingle Blunt, who came alongside me 55 years ago and has had my back ever since. Many will attest that she has made our home a place where dozens of young couples and countless others have found joy and peace with an amazing meal served along with her wisdom to savor. Her intellect, humor, hospitality, and our "truth in love" conversations during the lee of the day, and above all her amazing grace toward me, have made me a far better man than I ever could have been. I keep discovering in "the last of life for which the first was made" that God gave me the best mentor I ever could hope for, someone who prayed this book into existence. Let's persist together with zeal until we are home.

ELDERS AT THE GATE
A CALL TO REPAIR THE GENERATIONAL LINKS

Broken hands on broken ploughs
Broken treaties, broken vows
Broken pipes, broken tools
People bending broken rules
Hound dog howling, bullfrog croaking
Everything is broken[1]

Bob Dylan

Certain things stick in your mind; others seem to just fade away. You probably know this by now. Among those we remember, just a few become touchstones for life. That's what happened when someone first called me, "Sir." It hit me right out of the blue without any warning. That innocuous greeting started something that has not stopped—not yet anyway. That is the day I began to become an elder.

It happened in the most mundane way. I was in a hardware store simply nosing around among the aisles of tools. The young man's salutation was obviously not because I held a higher rank or had some superior position. It definitely was not because I'm what you would call distinguished looking. Hardly. No, it was apparently just a courteous remark by a younger man to well—OK, an *older* man—what I've now come to call an elder. All I could conclude at the time was that I must have looked as if I deserved

1

it. But later I began to see it as a bit of a turning point in my life and not simply something amusing to share with B.J., my wife. In retrospect, it quietly launched the time when I think I first began to say to myself, "I'm getting old!"

So, it was not simply an off the cuff remark on my part when our good friend, Anne, upon turning a certain age, received this e-mail consolation from me: "Well, Anne, now you can take your place as an elder at the gate!" It turns out we are not the first to be caught up in this question of what our role is once we draw near to being the elders.

At the Gate

In ancient times, the city gate was where people went for judicial decisions, for counsel, and to gather the latest news. Those who were no longer able to go off to the fields, to their shops, or to the market to work, spent much of their time sitting by the gates of the city. They were not there just to play checkers, watch haircuts, or gossip. They assumed their places as other elders had before them, taking up their necessary role reserved for them. This was a key societal position, one expected of them as they became the next keepers and dispensers of judicious wisdom to the coming generations. Without city gates, perhaps we have lost something we didn't even know we were missing; something essential to a good life even—a place to go for wisdom, a purpose to fulfill for those who are aging, an accessible and established link to the generations that follow. It all connected.

Where do those younger go for wisdom today? Google; Wikipedia; YouTube for starters. That's about the size of it.

What is the purpose for those who have years of life ahead? Retirement? Golf? Fifty-five and over perpetual care communities? It's not clear at all.

What about the nature of our culture today? How well do the generations connect, older with younger, without city gates?

As Bob Dylan reminds us, it appears something is broken, and sometimes it does feel like "everything." As an elder I simply want to focus on just one thing that has become very clear to me—*The young need anchoring in deep, adult connections; their elders need to rediscover their established purpose in their last lap—together they can restore the broken links of the design for a full, meaningful life as intended by their Creator.*

For those who are elders or can imagine themselves as such one day, this challenge to mend is for us to take up the gauntlet. To do so, we need all the wisdom we can get, and for that it is best we begin to go back to the time when wisdom was prized and sought after, the role that awaited in a long-lived life.

ANCIENT WISDOM

First a word of context. I write this with a Christian worldview. I do so for two reasons. One, I'm a Christian and my questions about meaning in life, especially in my latter years, have never been answered by philosophy or sophistry but rather by what I believe is ancient wisdom. Not that I've lived wisely all my life, or even understood what wisdom is, but when I began to think about how to finish well as a "Sir," I found the questions best answered by what has stood the test of time, particularly in our "broken" age. Second, with the brokenness that is all around us, I find Judaism and Christianity, alone among the religions and even philosophies, have the most well thought out answers that are key to attend to the mending and life's meaning.

You don't have to be a Christian to consider this ancient wisdom for yourself, so as you read this if you are not religious, it's not intended to be a sneaky apologetic. I hope tried and true wisdom can be respected by people of all beliefs or those with no particular belief. In fact, I will make the case that the Christian church may be among the worst offenders in this brokenness by ignoring how societies like ours can live wisely connected—younger to older—despite what are their good intentions. That may make Christians uncomfortable, but I'd encourage them to hang in there with me, too.

3

The backdrop then for what lies ahead is to understand the loss of the meaning of wisdom—head and heart—and its necessity for our times in connecting the generations, gate or no gate, and the role for wise elders at a time when the aging population is growing rapidly. How that plays out remains to be seen in the pages ahead.

Now to wisdom. With the very opening lines of Solomon's great gathering of Near East acumen in the ancient book of Proverbs, we hear the earnest advice of the female protagonist, Wisdom. Her timeless critique speaks immediately to our 21st Century culture about the missing role of the elders and the implications of disconnection with those who are in the early stages of life. As she enters the scene, she begins to walk along the noisy streets of Jerusalem, calling loudly for the people to follow her to the gates where she gives this ominous warning:

> *Because I have called and you refused to listen, have stretched out my hand and no one has heeded, because you have ignored all my counsel and would have none of my reproof, I also will laugh at your calamity; I will mock when terror strikes you.*[2]

At first blush, we might be tempted to read the message as: "You young kids, you better pay attention to the older folks or you will make bad choices and all hell will break loose." But Wisdom goes to the gates because it is the *elders* who are not there; they are failing to build a relationship with her and it is their hearts, that deepest human place within each of us, not just their heads, that suffer. As a result, they do not play their needed role, the generational links are breaking down, and the young suffer the most. For Israel, disaster actually would follow Solomon's generation as his own son ignored this admonition.

Wisdom says to each generation down through the years, it is not your responsibility as elders to garner a comfy seat while others pass by and give you honorific greetings, nor is it yours to find a warm place to end your days after selling your snow shovels as you head south.

The intent of Wisdom is not for elders to be exclusively with people who look like us once our time for productive contribution is all but ended. As we grow older, she does not want us to just withdraw into our 55-and-over continuous care entertainment zones, devoid of the noise and messiness of little kids, while we watch amusing digital images as our last act. To be sure, walking the fairways of well-manicured golf courses on occasion is certainly a good form of exercise and camaraderie, but our culture's image of retirement can also become a deadly trap, even setting the stage for terror to enter at our gates. The implications for our culture are as poorly understood today as they were 3,000 years ago. Perhaps we can recapture these ancient insights.

In a nutshell, the narrative ahead is for those who can envision themselves as one day receiving their fiftieth birthday gifts of an AARP card and a colonoscopy, as well as those who are already there: you will be, or are, a needed though often missing source of wisdom in a broken world where the generational links have been badly strained. This is also for those emerging adults[3] who are already on their frantic way to and fro, seeking direction for the beginning of their life story: those who sit by the gate are the secret sauce. That is ancient wisdom, not modern pride. If you are not quite an elder, but no longer young, consider this an early wake-up call that you will be an elder one day, and know you can learn to take advantage of what those that go before you have to offer without remaking their mistakes.

ADULTING

If there is one symptom of this brokenness it is captured in the exaggerated media portrayal of the rising generation. In a combination of disdain and dark humor, emerging adults, Millennials,[4] are usually depicted as narcissists, gamers, and slackers, marked by a self-absorbed fixation with screens and digital amusement as they travel with their loose tribe. This is the view that many who are older imagine is accurate where the young are freeloaders in their parents' basements, delaying "adulting"[5] as long as possible. As in all caricatures there is some truth here, but it masks the actual heightened anxiety, depression, and sense of loneliness in those who are becoming adults that are genuine symptoms of what is lost. We are not seeing some evolutionary quirk or personal failure in delayed adulthood.

To be sure, many of the young are doing just fine. Still, it is fair to say many who are younger would covet a few older people who would sit down and simply hear them out and give them some wise advice rather than criticize. They are the product of those who are elders, and elders have a need to acknowledge we can do far better. So, this is neither a critique of those older or younger but rather a look into the nature of our times and how we can come together to better achieve God's original design for a good life. I hope to show just how that can play out.

LISTEN

This story is an encouragement for us all to do what Wisdom asks of us: listen to her as she speaks to our day, a time not only of actual, looming terror at the very gates of our great cities, but a time of great social divide. Whether it is in education, poverty, race, culture, immigration, sex, or living conditions, a caustic, nearly feckless political divide besets our leaders. Anxiety and depression seem almost a pandemic. All this fragmentation and even misery is compounded by deepening moral instability led by a hyper individualism and its handmaiden, ethical relativity.

In the pages ahead, we come to understand the life challenges among those in their teens through their 30s as well as those who realize their younger days lie behind. Both have questions, good questions, that have wise answers encapsulated in the lost purpose and role for elders. It is not just our national leadership in all sectors which seems to grow even more dysfunctional in the new millennium: that is too easy of a target and too simple an excuse we have been making. For those of us now addressed as "sir" or "ma'am," the symptoms of cultural and societal decline have grown exponentially just within our lifetimes—and we are implicated. We who came of age in post-World War II America have seen it all happen and it's been on our watch.

THE ROAD AHEAD

The fundamental story here is to explain why there is a need to restore the generational links and thus to recover the strategy God devised long ago for the older generation in shaping the next with the wisdom of life's experiences and relationships. This he intends for the good of a society that might otherwise remain broken. The meaningful role for elders is one God has envisioned and it is ours to recover.

In Chapter 1, Two Paths, we begin the story by seeing that our culture has a well-worn, well-advertised path for the retirement years best characterized by the "bucket list"—finally getting to do all the things that leisure and life savings can provide, often in a more benign climate. However, there is a second path, the one less often followed, and it is the discovery of the power of purpose in bringing in a heart of wisdom and engaging in the unique vocation reserved for the "third third"[6] of life we discuss next.

In Chapter 2, Finishing Well, we begin with a vision for this third third, one of living the remaining years with zeal for the task prepared for us and for our response to the role that life and God has prepared for us to do: wise mentors who build deep relationships with the next generation. This is the first link to strengthen.

In Chapter 3, Miserable and Unprepared: What's Wrong with these Kids? we look at the second link, the generations coming behind, generally referred to as the Millennials and Gen Z (or the iGen) in order to understand how these emerging adults are different, challenged by many factors their elders did not face. One particular characteristic is the well-documented decline in their faith. Another is the delay in maturity. Alongside these lie the accelerated rise in the psychological pains of anxiety and depression

7

which are at unprecedented levels, and the new "diseases of despair" which beset them as they grow older. All these are symptoms that something has been broken.

Chapter 4, Who Trained the Canaries to Sing?, seeks an understanding of how elders were shaped in *their* youth, which get us closer to the root causes that disrupted our generational connections. The central metaphor introduced here is one of "adult abandonment," the most pungent source of the generational weakening already described. Paradoxically, this is also the key to understanding the mending process. This concludes the first part of the book with the table set for rediscovering the ancient design for elders at the gate—that of mentors.

The takeaway from the first part of this story is hopefully an honest, but not overly simplistic picture of the generations, older and younger, not a condemnation of either those of us with gray hair or of those who are becoming freshly-minted adults. In the second half, we lay out the vision, a more fulsome and encouraging vision for connecting older and younger than either our culture or the church has generally offered, through stories of elders and those younger who are demonstrating the ancient wisdom meant by the term, "Elders at the gate."

In Chapter 5, Mentors Are MIA, we turn to the scriptures for fleshing out the vision for how to live a good, full life and to build a good society; here is contained the knowledge of how to recover the lost wisdom of solid relationships between generations. This is a picture as fresh now as it was then. Ironically, as we will see, this message is as much for the church and how seniors are seen there, as it is for our culture and how it views aging. The message for the church and for the secular culture alike is that the ancient wisdom envisions that elders are not meant to "go gentle into that good night"[7] but to play the role elders have been prepared for: wise mentors to the next generations.

In Chapter 6, The Culture for Growing Mentors, we see that the circumstances in which great mentors are best grown is one that is intergenerational. Even though mentoring is most often associated with the workplace, it is actually the church which is the ideal place in which we learn to be the mentors and elders that God intended for us to become and in which the generational links are best strengthened. One example of how this is done is offered for visualization.

In Chapter 7 we read several Stories from Those Who Pass by the Gate. These are told by a number of people who describe just what their mentors did that made such an impact in their lives through heart relationships. Over and over, we find there are three central themes that emerge. If you understand at this point in the story why this role of mentor is the design for the latter portion of life, then these stories provide the view from where a younger person sits—not as a "how to" guide, but rather "why to," garnered from experience.

Then in Chapter 8 we read the Stories from Those Who Sit at the Gate. These are tales drawn from the other end of the telescope, from the point of view of seven exemplary older people who come together in a metaphorical "council of elders" to tell of their experiences in mentoring singles, young marrieds, men, and women. These are individuals who have discovered the joy in this work and have a passion that is contagious. Here readers night better envision possible ways to take up their place at the gate as mentors. This is not a checklist but an array of practical lessons drawn from personal narratives: insights that mostly elude bullet points. In other words, it is shared wisdom.

Before closing, Chapter 9, "So What Am I Supposed to Do... and Not Do?," addresses the kind of questions that may be remaining—those I am often asked about mentoring. As some final, practical thoughts on how to get started, you can apply them with individuals, in a church or organization, in small groups, or with your spouse and other couples. The form this takes for you can vary as much as the needs within the relationships you already have or within the community that already exists around you. All that remains is to get on with being that elder at the gate, either now or when the time comes, and to do your part in the ancient and wise plan to connect each generation to the next.

Before we begin, let me share one story that might help make the picture you have a bit clearer. It is a story told by my good friend, Anne, offered as an encouragement to you to keep reading.

So... It was August. It was hot. We were in the deep South, having traveled with a loaded van from the relative cool of the DC area. Task at hand: drop first-born child at college for his freshman experience. If I'd only known the first thing about how to do this: help him unpack or leave him to it? Take him out to eat or let him get 'into' the situation? Cry or don't cry? Look at the austere room and commiserate or comfort and find the bright side? I was paralyzed with confusion and I didn't have a clue about what to do. I'd not thought to ask anyone who'd been there ahead of me and at that time I couldn't think of anyone in my life like that anyway. For some weird reason, all I could see was the incredible kudzu that was growing everywhere down in this hot and steamy land. It creeped me out. I'd heard that a tendril of it could climb up the side of a car in the span of an overnight. That seemed scary, but not helpful I knew. I didn't mention it.

The sad part for me was that I didn't have a bench of wise people "at the gate" to ask. I'd at least liked to have figured out my questions: "How do you do this? I know this is a big deal. What do I need to be thinking about as I am (literally) dropping him off for this huge step? What's the main thing I should be communicating to him beyond tears? Is there even a THING that's a main thing, or maybe I just need to keep quiet? I don't know!" I was lost.

And so, the poor kid just got what he got from me: a sad, flustered, weepy parent who didn't know how to help him that day. As he bravely started to set up housekeeping, I helped a little by organizing, but I couldn't decide if this was helping him or was I just being annoying. I don't remember the rest of the day other than driving away feeling both terrible and inadequate.

CHAPTER 1

TWO PATHS

To finish the moment, to find the journey's end in every step of the road, to live the greatest number of good hours, is wisdom.... Since our office is with moments, let us husband them.[8]

So teach us to number our days that we may get a heart of wisdom.[9]

Common wisdom in the secular age tells us that on the journey of life we had best pay attention to what occurs along the way; don't worry so much about the destination. I suppose there is something to that, not always being concerned about the future, rather appreciate today lest we miss something important. Still, when we who are made in God's image sense we are nearer to that end, we inevitably begin to ask ourselves, "How do I do this? What is the wisest way to live so that things end well? Do I even know where I am going?" Ernest Becker tells us that we begin to ask these questions because each person who has ever walked the earth engages in a delicate mental dance that on the one hand denies death, yet on the other cannot deter that awareness completely. That sure sense we will one day die is what catches up the wise and the fool alike. We are that animal that knows there is an end.[10] Knowing that, we can choose to avoid the thought or we can choose to take it seriously. Wisdom, Godly wisdom, says we live responsibly, not morbidly, to the very end.

11

Over the centuries, the question of how to finish life well has been answered in a number of different ways. The great Russian writer, Leo Tolstoy, told the story *Two Old Men*[11] to suggest one answer as he tells of two men and two paths.

It seems Efim and Elisha, friends of years and friends of tears, were nearing the end of their lives; they had made a pact to accomplish one last task together before they died. As old men often do, their thoughts had turned toward spiritual matters. In their day, a pilgrimage to Jerusalem was the capstone for many devout Russians, and so it was they said goodbye to their families and gathered their provisions to set out on the long road. But, as all stories and life journeys do, this one soon presented them with a crisis.

After several days they came upon a small hut which looked at first glance to have been abandoned recently. But upon closer observation they found that plague and starvation had invaded the tiny homestead and that a father, mother, and two children along with an old grandmother lay near death. Efim was reluctant to stop because it seemed obvious they would die anyway, but Elisha decided to tarry to do what he could for them and said he would catch up later. That proved to be a life-changing decision, the place where the story and the two men's last journey diverged.

Over the next days, Elisha succeeded in reviving the family, remaining with them until they could get back on their feet. When it came time to leave and to catch up with Efim, the little ones clung to his legs and cried pitifully that they had no horse to work the field and no cow for milk for they had been sold. In his empathy, one thing led to another and by the time it was all through, Elisha had expended almost all of his life savings and realized his pilgrimage was at an end. He could only turn back toward home, his spiritual quest ended.

Meanwhile, Efim went on his way to Jerusalem and experienced the highlight of the pilgrimage they had long imagined—worshiping at the midnight mass at the Sepulcher of Christ. Yet, it was here the oddest thing happened. Pushed forward amidst the large crowd, he was stunned to see the distinctive bald head of his friend, Elisha, arms outstretched as if a priest at the altar. But by the time he wove his way forward, Elisha had disappeared into the crowd—or so it seemed. Though he looked everywhere, he never found him among the pilgrims.

Still perplexed on his journey to return home, Efim came to the very village where he and Elisha had parted a year earlier. As he walked by, he was besieged by a young child to turn aside and rest. After dinner that evening, sitting before a good fire they told him the story of a stranger who rescued them when their end was near.

Had he not come we should all have died in our sins. We were dying in despair, murmuring against God and man. But he set us on our feet again; and through him we learned to know God and to believe that there is good in man, May the Lord bless him! We used to live like animals, he made human beings of us.[12]

It was then Efim realized that it was Elisha whose sacrificial offering of service to those in need had been accepted by God. At the end, Tolstoy leaves the reader to ponder with Efim what God's purpose is for man at the end of his life. To Tolstoy the answer is clear: "Show love and do good to others,"[13] leave the world with your legacy secured in the lives of others. What makes this such a classic story is that Tolstoy wrestles with the question we all must face, now or later. *What does it mean to finish life well? What meaning is there when our life's work seemingly comes to an end?* None of us can be indifferent to these questions simply because it is not a matter of indifference to the God who created us. The choices we make when we approach the last phase of our lives make all the difference in how that question is answered. Two paths are offered.

The Bucket List

For most of us, in the prosperous West at least, we talk about our *bucket list* as the remaining things we want to accomplish before we finish. Of course, those choices, as we plan ahead for our retirement, begin with financial planning, for we reason it all depends on how long the money lasts. If we live long, we want to ensure a good closing scene, and we are awash in advice on how best to prepare. Retirement seminars and financial advisors are widely consulted: "Can we make it on what we have saved?" we ask. Planning for sufficient finances is certainly the number one contemporary measure of how we ensure our life ends well. This is our culture's notion of preparing for the best end in our golden years.

Others ponder, where? Many people begin to research the list of the ten best places to retire where weather and cost of living and cultural amenities coincide in a perfect storm of worry-free living, likely with others their age, perhaps with reasonable proximity to grandchildren thrown in.

Once the decisions are made about finances and whether to put down new roots, then typically we are encouraged to turn to those new experiences we've waited a long time for. While most of us may not plan to make a spiritual pilgrimage, it is generally accepted that this is a time when the postponed opportunities are tackled. We may wish to travel to Israel, as Efim and Elisha did, or cruise to far off places, perhaps the Greek Isles or a river cruise in Europe if we've saved our pennies. Others have waited to take up a hobby in earnest or to build something. Then there is recreation, where the time to play more golf or tennis or even learn to play pickle ball fit in with the modern penchant to maintain youthful fitness as an end goal.

In essence, for many, the focus is on doing what we've long delayed and hoped to do in the last part of life—if our health holds up. But what often gnaws at us still is does this give our lives meaning as we prepare to take our places as elders? We instinctively know this is not all that it means to finish well.

THE POWER OF PURPOSE

As we grow older, we have this curious habit of beginning to look backwards while the younger generations are mostly looking forward to what lies ahead. It's not simply an orthopedic issue of the neck. We elders tend to reminisce more and to tell stories, often of our feckless youth. I think this is what Soren Kierkegaard, the Danish philosopher and theologian, was trying to get at when he said that "life is lived forward, but it can only be understood by looking backward."[14] The older we get the more we seek to *understand* our life for its meaning while the young seek to figure out what it is they are going to *do*. In other words, as elders we begin to understand ourselves in new ways but also to see more clearly that our lives' purpose has not run its course even if our major occupations draw toward closure. At the very least those younger seek to resolve issues elders have left behind, viz., what their major should be, who and when they should marry, and whether to take this job in this city or to pursue that advanced degree. The young can't wait to find out what *real* life is all about beyond school and whether they are up to it, perhaps not realizing preparation *is* real life. Elders on the other hand have lived that time, but now they begin to seek to connect the dots of their decades.

The Kierkegaard paradox is exactly what Richard Leider sought to gain insight into when he spent nearly 20 years interviewing older adults—people over 65 who had finished their careers— asking them deep questions that might reveal some lessons learned. The question that provided the greatest insights he found was this one: "If you could live your life over again, what would you do differently?" That is the polite question. The implicit question was, "What are your regrets? Where do you think you might have done better along the way?" Strikingly, he began to find there were three themes repeated over and over:

I would take the time for *reflection*, time to think and to savor life because it all passes by so quickly. I was just too busy *doing* to realize the need to appreciate it more.

I would be more courageous; take more *risks*; I played it too close to the vest.

I would be clear, far earlier, on understanding the ultimate *resolution* of my life—what my purpose was and how I would pursue it until the end.

Reflection. Risk. Resolution. Eventually Leider put these lessons into a small book, *The Power of Purpose*.[15] I'd suggest only one alteration to his thesis. In his presuppositions, he divides a full life into three time segments: (1) *school* and preparation where we ready ourselves to work and find our purpose; (2) *work* where we live out our purpose and find the deeper meaning in life; (3) *retirement* where we savor what we have done and enjoy all those things we didn't have time for. I would agree that for lives that now extend well into the eighties as the norm they are sorted into almost equal thirds. Where I part company with him is that the focus for the last third of the journey is retirement, or at least the modern understanding of what that phase constitutes, whether it is looking back to savor life or living the long delayed good life of adult day camp. That, I believe, is a recipe for missing out on what joy this time can hold, because purpose and career do not end together.

The focus played out in the rest of this book is what I will call the vocation of being an *elder at the gate*, the purpose for life when we've turned the corner and are heading for home. For those blessed with long years, there is a common destination: life does end, life on earth that is. But it is what path we choose to take that makes all the difference. We can either fall into the culture's bucket list route for us or we can re-discover the ancient purpose and the long-established role reserved for those as they grow older and somewhat wiser as a better way. To do so we must debunk a common misunderstanding: the role of elder at the gate is rooted deeply in who we are created to be as human beings made in the image of God. We are meant, prepared really, for a life in full. In short:

The three-phase scenario for a purposeful life, one which ends in a final season of experiencing the rewards of delayed gratification, is a common, widely accepted misunderstanding. Instead, there is a

16

far better way to approach this last part of the journey and that is to discover our lasting and perhaps most important vocation. The closing life purpose for elders is to gain a heart of wisdom and to mentor those coming behind with the gift of deep relationships as extensively as our capacities allow, right up until the end.

RECAPTURING YOUTH

Along with the choice of two possible paths as we grow older lies a cultural trap that is unique to our times. It is our attitude toward the older years that is two sides of the same coin: both are seductive. On the one hand, we are told we must avoid aging because it only leads to ugliness and death; on the other we are advised not only to deter the advances of time but to seek a return to youth. The reigning assumption behind both of culture's views is that growing older and experiencing the ravages of age is to be avoided as long as possible. Given modern medicine and the emerging science surrounding aging bodies and brains, many now opt for ways to keep at bay what has formerly been viewed as the normal course of life. Surgery, injections, special diets, pills, exercise (body and brain), and lifestyle choices are fast becoming an economic niche industry designed to create a demand in the rapidly growing older demographic to hold onto youth.

As a late in life high school teacher, I am often told that, "Those kids must really keep you young." I am often tempted to say, "No, actually it's the opposite—they remind me how old I am and how much I need to pass on what they cannot yet know." This hearkening back to youth is not as new a phenomenon as one might think. In his poem, *Ulysses*, Tennyson imagines an aging Odysseus wrestling with his last years alongside his wife Penelope whom he had once yearned for during his long journeys, then fought for upon his return. But now as an old man, his longing is to leave her and once again, as when he was young, sail off with a hearty crew, leaving his responsibilities to his son, Telemachus. He has no desire to age in place.

17

How dull it is to pause, to make an end,
To rust unburnish'd, not to shine in use!
As tho' to breathe were life! Life piled on life
Were all too little, and of one to me
Little remains: but every hour is saved
From that eternal silence, something more,...

He speaks then to his old cronies and puts before them one last great adventure:

Free hearts, free foreheads—you and I are old;
Old age hath yet his honour and his toil;
Death closes all: but something ere the end,
Some work of noble note, may yet be done,
Not unbecoming men that strove with Gods.
The lights begin to twinkle from the rocks:
The long day wanes: the slow moon climbs: the deep
Moans round with many voices. Come, my friends,
'Tis not too late to seek a newer world.

What Tennyson keenly imagines is not so much that the old adventurer wants to avoid aging, but what Odysseus really wants is to recapture that sense of purpose and meaning he felt in days gone by when he and Penelope were at the height of their powers. Simply staying to "rust unburnish'd" as the elders do at the gate will not suffice for him.

Push off, and sitting well in order smite
The sounding furrows; for my purpose holds
To sail beyond the sunset, and the baths
Of all the western stars, until I die.
It may be that the gulfs will wash us down:
It may be we shall touch the Happy Isles,
And see the great Achilles, whom we knew.

Tho' much is taken, much abides; and tho'
We are not now that strength which in old days
Moved earth and heaven, that which we are, we are;
One equal temper of heroic hearts,
Made weak by time and fate, but strong in will
To strive, to seek, to find, and not to yield.

The challenge before us is *not* to yield to this vision others have for us, rather we need to push on beyond the siren call of perpetual youth, revisiting the so-called glory days when we felt we had a purpose. To see our purpose for the latter years as being our bucket list closing act is the road to ending life with disappointment. Instead, let us find the vocation, the meaning designed for us for the third third. For that we turn next to one of my mentors.

As someone even older than I am, I do consider him an elder at the gate for us, even though I've only seen him speak one time. He has taught me a lesson which is worth passing on, one that will be the beginning point for our framework of what finishing well might look like. He's what I'd call an old saint who has words of wisdom for those who have arrived at the gate or for those who can imagine one day having accumulated threescore years and ten.

CHAPTER 2

FINISHING WELL

The time of my departure has come. I have fought the good fight, I have finished the race, I have kept the faith. Henceforth there is laid up for me the crown of righteousness, which the Lord, the righteous judge, will award to me on that day, and not only to me but also to all who have loved his appearing.[16]

Zeal, says J.I. Packer is what ought to characterize the life of an elder. But he begins with this reality: "We grow old."[17] Great, how many reminders do we need? Yet, somehow this forthright truth often comes as a mild surprise to each one of us blessed by living to see our grandchildren, the appearance of arthritis, and fading or falling hair. Denial needs to be revealed first.

While Packer falls into the self-described "oldest old" category—those he marks as above 85—his audience is those of us who are merely older, or becoming aware of it. The heart of the message he brings that I find spot on is to file a protest about the assumptions of our culture (and, regrettably, the church)—that the elderly are to be the recipients of the services of others now that their productive years lie behind. Social Security and Medicare, for example, use the mid-sixties in their outdated annuity calculations, and the implication is you're at an age where you need help from Uncle Sam. In essence, Packer calls this bunk and paints a far more encouraging picture.

He begins with a passage from Psalm 92, clearly written by an elder:

They still bear fruit in old age;
they are ever full of sap and green,
to declare that the Lord is upright;
he is my rock.[18]

His emphasis is that a good old age is time intended not to lie fallow but for fruitfulness—this is God's expectation. Packer's thesis lies at the heart of the theme we are pursuing.

"[S]o far as our bodily health allows," he says, "we should aim to be found running the last lap of the race of our Christian life, as we would say, flat out. The final sprint, so I urge, should be a sprint indeed."[19] He recognizes that this contrasts sharply with what many Americans assume is the normal and mature thing to do—slow down, relax, enjoy your life; you've earned a rest. Such thinking is not only misguided, he says, it is a temptation unique to the latter years, one that lurks within the good intentions of many, even churches, which often reinforces this misperception with their programs for those older.

In undoubted kindness, he says, churches seek to do good for their seniors when they offer senior ministries to help this constituency enjoy their golden years in the company of others their age. Thus, typically, the church caters to the elderly with small trips, social events, luncheons, camaraderie, and book discussions. Certainly these help alleviate the loneliness that older people often face. But he says this is also "one of the huge follies of our time." It is an approach, he believes, which deserves to be unmasked as being unbiblical, narcissistic, and a squandering of all that God has built into one's life for such a time as this.

Other than the humility borne of accepting bodily limits and loss of societal status, Packer says there is a vocation intended for the final phase of life. It begins simply by "keeping going." He is not necessarily advocating busyness, staying on the job until you are carted out of your cubicle or seeking one last hurrah of triumph in building a bigger monument to yourself. Transitions do naturally occur he agrees, but the modern idea of retirement to a daily life of non-stop recreation is not God's vision for us.

Anyone older than 65, or who can see 65 approaching, needs to start thinking about and planning for what lies ahead, he says. For those last 20 or 30 remaining years (using current statistics on life span), he sees God using this third phase to hone and buff us into Christ's likeness before calling us home, and that means we are also "sent" as he was. This is what Moses means in Psalm 90, we earnestly ask God to "teach us to number our days," to use this time well, so that we "gain" or "bring in" a heart of wisdom. *Wisdom is not so much being able to give good advice but by the last phase of life to have a heart more and more like Christ so that when we share our lives his presence in our deep relationships helps others to be more like him.* That is much of our purpose in the latter days.

Citing Billy Graham, Packer affirms with him that the word "retire" is not recorded in the Bible nor is anything akin to it extolled as our ending purpose. The great heroes of the faith finish the race well, bursting the tape as I was taught when beginning to run the quarter mile in high school. We are not simply to jog the last steps when fatigue grabs legs and lungs with hearts that beat less vigorously and more flutteringly. He summarizes:

> *In personal terms, this winding down may seem natural enough. Not only has the world pensioned them off; they are starting to feel that their bodies are running out of steam, so that reducing the demands they make of themselves is appropriate self-care. By moving us to think this way, however, Satan undermines, diminishes, and deflates our discipleship, reducing us from laborers in Christ's kingdom to sympathetic spectators, and as such passengers whom the congregation carries by means of the exertions of others.*[20]

For my wife B.J. and I, we recognize here is where the tension lies for us and for many of our peers. Many argue and even assume that if we have the health, and if we have the means, why shouldn't we enjoy what we couldn't in our more constrained youth? After

23

a life of work don't we owe it to ourselves to take a nap or a long lunch or travel widely?

Packer says, *No*, not as our primary purpose at least. This freedom in life choices provides, for example he says, the opportunity for serious catechetical (not simply devotional) Bible study and providing intergenerational leadership in the church and elsewhere by influencing younger persons' lives with wisdom and caring. I'd also add this is a message meant for today's church in their strategic thinking, not just for the life choices of individuals.

Thus, Packer returns to *zeal*, urging us to finish the race this way. This uncommon word is how he describes the attitude toward life we ought to demonstrate despite our years. In fact, he says, zeal is a word God uses to describe *himself* and is also the way Jesus approached the cross—with a zeal for the Kingdom.

Zeal is not a precursor to just another form of burnout, he says, because the Scriptures promise that the Holy Spirit will renew us. Nowhere does the Bible suggest that such energies are confined to those below a certain age.[21]

The implication he leaves us with is that particularly in old age vigorous work and faithful commitments are acts of faith fueled by our ultimate hope in the one who gives us zeal, God himself. We attend to *heart work* as we number our days and then share our lives and our hearts with those that are coming after.

CONTENTMENT?

One day as I was finishing Packer's little gem of a book, I was reminded of a sunny, warm kayak ride I had taken a few weeks earlier while on vacation in Florida. Setting out from the dock, I paddled by one large boat after another, all lined up in front of beautiful condos sitting along the channels leading out into the bay. I began to notice that many of these boats had names that spoke of their owner's hope for the good life ahead: *Dad's Dream*; *Finally*; *No Egrets*; and *Last Office*. The one that really caught my eye was a particularly large boat emblazoned with *Contentment* as its owner's self-expression. As I looked up at this massive craft, I found myself wondering, "Is this guy really content now?" Not only was it a cash-eating cow that a young, shirtless man was attending to for his patron, but there it sat, gathering barnacles and the deterioration that accompanies any idle boat. A metaphor perhaps?

As hard as it may be, even in old age we are called to, prepared for, and needed by those who come after us. Thus we are called to persist, we do have a purpose yet, a calling or vocation for this time, and so we run—preferably with zeal. Indeed, we are to run and keep running until we hear Christ say, "Well done." In that we can be content. But there is some attention to ourselves that *does* deserve to be followed if these years are to be fruitful and we are to finish well.

ONE THING I DO

If anyone had his eye on the prize at the end of life, it was the apostle Paul. Repeatedly he sounds this theme of a good finish to life—sometimes as encouragement to his readers to persist; sometimes it seems he is reinforcing the message for himself. Under house arrest in Rome, he writes to readers in and around Philippi and makes clear his singular focus as he looks to his days remaining:

> *I count all things to be loss in view of the surpassing value of knowing Christ Jesus my Lord, for whom I have suffered the loss of all things, and count them but rubbish so that I may gain Christ, and may be found in Him, not having a righteousness of my own derived from the Law, but that which is through faith in Christ, the righteousness which comes from God on the basis of faith, that I may know Him and the power of His resurrection and the fellowship of His sufferings, being conformed to His death; in order that I may attain to the resurrection from the dead.*[22]

His concern is for his *heart*, the deepest most mysterious place that is the essence of our image-of-God humanity. He wants to *know* Christ, in an intimacy that exceeds that of marriage; to have such a deep relationship that he may experience his power and even his sufferings that one day he, too, may be resurrected with him. This is not for his own self-aggrandizement but that his heart filled with the knowledge and wisdom of Christ may be shared.

We see this later, when Paul, awaiting execution in a Roman prison, writes perhaps his last letter addressed to his young protégé, Timothy. Here he seems to reach back to this earlier intent, that of his life's purpose: in finishing with the a zeal for and a focus on Christ, he wants to pass this passion on to his protégé. "I have fought the good fight, I have finished the race, I have kept the faith."[23] As God's inspired word to us elders, it is a truth we can take to the bank by living it out in our race as well. More to the point, what does it look like to finish well?

In our time, perhaps no one has studied this question more than Bobby Clinton, a Fuller Seminary professor, who is best known for his examination of how leaders are formed and how they progress at various stages of life.[24] In looking at the journey of many Christian leaders over the course of their lives, he made a surprising discovery—many, in fact, did *not* finish well. The usual suspects, the gods of our times—power, sex, money, pride—account for much of where elders fall short of the line. But severe family issues, mental plateauing, and running out of steam are also factors he cites. As he began to dig beneath this, he identified six factors that are important for us to understand if we would sit beside the gate as responsible elders and live life with a zeal toward a good last chapter:

1. Maintain a vibrant and deeply personal spiritual relationship with God to the very end.

2. Remain a continuous learner from life experiences and from humbly learning from others, especially those who are younger.

3. Become progressively more Christlike in character, with a life that evidences such virtues (fruit is the oft-used metaphor).

4. Continue to live a life of truth where the convictions of obedience and trust in the promises of God are seen to be

real, particularly in the hardships old age inevitably brings.

5. Leave behind one or more contributions (legacy is the popular term—but for God's glory, not self), in the lives of others.

6. Live with a growing sense of purpose or destiny that may or may not be seen as fully accomplished in one's lifetime.[25]

As I've reflected on these myself, what I've realized is that while focused zeal is crucial, above all I need to guard my heart while I continue to grow—I have not yet arrived at who I want to be. My relationship with the One who gave all he had right to the very end of his life, needs to grow and deepen even as my body now feeling aching shoulders and lessening energy declines. In fact, as we consider our calling late in life, I wonder if we can't turn these bodily losses into strengths.

DECLINE IS INEVITABLE, BUT...

My wife and I recently finished reading a very important book about this dilemma, *On Mortality* by Atul Gawande.[26] We feel it is a must read which we keep pressing on our friends. The key point the author makes is the truth which we must contend with here: decline is written into our DNA despite the false lure of perpetual youth by our culture. As a physician, Gawande is candid that even with exercise, the Mediterranean Diet, statins, stretching, tai chi, relaxation exercises, and CoQ10, the physiological trajectory of life is that things go south. It's inevitable. The things we have come to love about our marvelous bodies—seeing, hearing, smelling, tasting, touching, balancing, strength, mobility, flexibility, memory, sleep, and even our moods—these all are subject to progressive and downward change. It's the Second Law of Thermodynamics writ large on our bodies. We who are elders know this, for we live it every day. Maintaining youth is a temptation that can only lead to despair, for it is a false idol. But what if we can begin to see these changes as opportunities for age-appropriate roles?

Cicero, in his remarkable essay *On Old Age*, offers an apologetic to the young about the shortcomings of age which they perceive lies ahead. As to physical decline, he says he did not desire the strength of a bull when young, so why should he want to be like a youthful athlete when he is old? Instead he says, "It is becoming to make use of what one has, and whatever you do, to do in proportion to your strength."[27] What if in God's wisdom, he uses our lessening capacities to an advantage, a *necessity* even to the role he has given us for the last lap? Certainly this is consistent with so many paradoxes in scripture where apparent weaknesses are in reality made into strengths. The central paradox, of course, is that in Christ's death emerges life eternal. If this principal of paradox is applied to old age as Cicero does, our latter time can become a cause for optimism as we look ahead.

Paul seems to speak to this reality in living when he says, "Though our outer self is wasting away, our inner self is being renewed day by day. For this light momentary affliction is preparing for us an eternal weight of glory beyond all comparison, as we look not to the things that are seen but to the things that are unseen. For the things that are seen are transient, but the things that are unseen are eternal."[28] Physical decline may say to us "You're over the hill, give it a rest, let others do it." But the truth is this may be our finest hour when all that has gone before is our preparation for what will culminate in a rousing final act. The world may never fully appreciate it, but if done wisely, it will be applauded one day where and by whom it counts. That is why I've come to appreciate the admonition "*persist*" above most others in scripture and elsewhere. That seems to sum up God's vision for the older generation's role and purpose, shrunk into one word. With this in mind, we are going to turn to what this can look like for elders. There is a need I believe only we can fill. As a bridge to where we are going, here is one final question, one that was posed to me which I still struggle a bit to answer nearly as well as Cicero did.

What Is It Like to be Old?

The question surprised me. Given the circumstances, it *really* surprised me. I was standing, naked, about to take a shower or, more precisely, I was standing with a young fellow who was about to give me the first assisted shower of my entire life or at least since I was a toddler.

A week before I had been doing something I've done for over forty years, I was out riding my bike for exercise and for the joy of being in the sun on a nice day, feeling the wind on my body and the strength in my legs. I remember distinctly I was accelerating down a slight hill then quickly decided to sharply turn onto a side street. I next woke up in an ambulance with someone fastening a collar firmly around my neck. What happened in between I was only able to partially reconstruct later. But the consequences were clear: seven broken ribs, a concussion, and a partially punctured lung.

What followed after the ER diagnosis was four days in the hospital then six days at a nursing home/rehabilitation center. This was the site of my assisted shower and the oddly timed question. The young man was African, from Ghana he said, in the U.S. for only six months. So when he asked, "What is it like to be old?" I was taken aback and found myself at a loss for an answer. I think I tried some lame humor about how you heal a lot more slowly, but that was not his point. He said that the reason he asked was that where he came from those who were old were given great respect. But he had found here in America that young people did not listen to those who were older and they definitely did not respect their wisdom. I had to think about that. I tried to answer him as best I could however. He really wanted to know.

I told him, honestly I had not ever given much thought to what it was like to be old. It just "is what it is" as we often say. But no, I told him, I have not experienced disrespect, at least not very often and that mostly when driving in impatient Washington DC traffic. From teaching high school the last eight years and from our mentoring of young couples before marriage, our experience with the next generation has been nothing but positive. But I told him

I thought I understood why he would say that for not everyone who is older has had our experience.

Still, it made me wonder, is it possible that many elders disengage from responsibilities because they think they have little to offer once they are classified as old? Do they fear that any advice would be disregarded as irrelevant? Do they fear as one older friend told me she felt "invisible" when she attended a young church plant?

If the thought of likely disrespect is in the back of your mind, I think you will find what we discuss next to be particularly encouraging. We are not only challenged to finish well with zeal, but there is a generation coming behind, just waiting for their elders. That is the role for which we have been well prepared. Thus, we ought to try to understand them and where their needs lie. That is where we turn to next.

CHAPTER 3

MISERABLE AND UNPREPARED
WHAT'S WRONG WITH THESE KIDS?[29]

Kids! I don't know what's wrong with these kids today.
Kids! Who can understand anything they say?
Kids! They are disobedient, disrespectful oafs; noisy,
crazy, sloppy, lazy loafers,
And while we're on the subject... Kids! You can talk and
talk till your face is blue,
Kids! But they still do just what they want to do.
Why can't they be like we were, perfect in every way?
What's the matter with kids today?[30]

No one actually sounded the warning, "The Millennials are coming! The Millennials[30] are coming!" Perhaps they should have. These guys and gals are markedly different than any before them and they are causing perplexity for their elders. The first wave has already hit the workforce and the last is about to graduate from college. The head-shaking stories already abound. Close on their heels, is the first generation to be raised with smartphones from the time they were kids—the so-called iGen or Generation Z. They may have even more acute issues to face.

A video I recently received from a friend contained a lone comment that told it all: "It may be closer to the truth then we want to believe!"

See if you think so:

Job Interview

Amy, a young woman, shows up for her first IT job interview with her cell phone in her lap, texting while she talks to a very patient older man who begins by asking her about her technology background. "Excel? PowerPoint? Publisher?" She looks up cheerily and says somewhat disdainfully, "No, none of those. You know, just the big ones: "Snapchat, Instagram, Pinterest, Vimeo, Twitter!" So the interviewer goes on to explain that she will need to use some of that office software to do research and bring him the results in particular formats. To which she responds, "No problem, I've got that covered, I'll just ask Siri!" So he smiles patiently and then says "Ask Siri if you can get to work each day promptly at 8:00." She says, "I don't understand, who gets up at 8?" She goes on to explain that normally she stays up texting until 3 am and doesn't get to Starbucks until 10 so she really works best starting at 10:45. By now her interviewer is a bit flustered and tells her this does not look like a good fit. That brings an indignant reply, "Why are you being so totally negative? It's stressing me out and I just don't feel safe in here anymore. I'm afraid I may need to take a mental health day." When she then crankily asks to speak to the HR director, he tries to reasonably explain that he hasn't hired her yet. She leaps up in righteous anger, "What? Are you firing me?" Then abruptly turns around and walks out with a flip of her hand and her ponytail.[31]

This is the generation raised on "Do what you want to do; be what you want to be." "I like you just the way you are." "Everybody's a winner." And, "Just be yourself." But what many are saying today is, "Houston, we have a problem." You'll perhaps recognize this as the infamous understatement uttered by Jim Lovell in the film *Apollo 13* (as well as in real life).[32] Similarly, not to be minimizing it in any way, there is a deeper, wider, and far more portentous spiritual and cultural problem facing American youth and young

32

adults that threatens more than three astronauts and the American space program. It's a hard right of passage nowadays.

The question at the outset about those who are younger is this: "What is the nature of their problems?" More to the point, "Where do the roots of the problem lie?" The danger is always, of course, are we solving symptoms or we getting at root causes? In this chapter, we take up the first question of what the problem is and will hold off on the diagnosis until the following chapter—that's where we elders figure into their story. Why? Simply because we're in it together, like it or not. We want to understand them, not condemn them.

Perhaps, you may ask, "Why is this important for me?" Let me just say this—knowing that there is a problem always implicates us in some way, so you may not want to know. Assuming you do want to understand, the case to be made moving forward is that the question of vocation, of end of life purpose for us elders, lies precisely here with the generations that need us.

So, Is There Really a Problem?

By now, the portrait of the Millennials has pretty well been painted in the media, not just in caricatures like the fictitious job interview. Businesses are tearing their hair out as they seek to understand how to manage this new generation while many parents are perplexed about how to build a bonfire of motivation to help their older children get off the couch, out of the basement, and into the workforce. But drawing on extensive research by sociologists, psychologists, and even theologians there is a far more helpful understanding that has emerged. Let's separate truth from cartoon.

Most experts who have studied Millennials have observed they are the product, of among other things, the self-esteem movement that impacted parenting and education during their early lives. Awarding them the shorthand moniker, GenMe, has seemed a fitting label, since Millennials *as a group* are known for hyper-individualism or, in its extreme form, narcissism.

For example, even the Army decided to change its recruiting slogan to "An Army of One" to attract this new breed—with only muted success—2% join the military compared with 13% of Boomers at their age.[33] Such regimentation is not generally what GenMe goes looking for because they are also not prone to be rule followers or group joiners. They prefer self-entertainment and social interaction online far more than their predecessors primarily because they came of age when such technology first hit the market during their formative years. The iGen so far is even more devoted to online living with even higher levels of anxiety and loneliness. Stay tuned.

GenMe[34]

The culture of individualism has had its impact on every area of life for Millennials—including their faith. That is what has had many of us who know them so concerned about for several years now. Take one of my favorite students, Madison.[35] Now here was a young person of solid, well-expressed faith; yet, perhaps emblematic of the uniqueness of this younger generation, it came with some new twists. On the one hand, his views are unremarkably orthodox: Christ as the only path to God; traditional marriage is affirmed by Jesus and Paul as defined from the beginning of time; self-control in dating is what it means to love God and his good purposes thus, no cohabitation (despite 75+% of his peers' disagreement), etc. On the other hand, Madison has great sympathy for the underdog, and like most of his generation he favors gay relationships, transgender rights, taking pride in who you are is of first importance. Despite many traditional beliefs, he sees Christians as often being haters, hypocrites, unwelcoming, and too often unloving. To many this seems a strange admixture of obedience to scripture while championing individual choice as the standard for morality. As we will see, the issue of such duality among young adults is not uncommon and it runs even deeper in other areas of life.

If this is the paradoxical heart of the moral foundation in today's

34

Millennial culture and the litmus test for making right choices is whether it makes you happy or is inclusive, then you would expect this cultural moment to have an impact on the religious lives and ethical choices of younger Christians. That's exactly what has emerged in the last decade. As a grandparent, this shift has left me and my peers perplexed.

When I stopped teaching leadership to seminary students and other rising mid-career people a few years ago and began teaching high school students, I was very unsure that I could even reach older teens as a gray-haired former Air Force officer. I felt I needed to understand them and what was happening in their generation since my last teenager had left home over twenty years before. Thus, I began to do some research as well as talk with them. I'll distil it here because what I learned helped me understand what I was experiencing in the classroom discussions and in the hallways and after school. If you anticipate working with the next generation, you may be as surprised by some of this as I was.

HERE COME THE NONES

To begin, most of us are by now familiar with the fact that the number of adult Americans who identify themselves as religiously *unaffiliated* (also called "Nones") has been growing rapidly. This category includes atheists, agnostics, and those who are following nothing in particular. While not approaching the dimensions of the demise of Christian affiliation in much of Europe, nevertheless U.S. religious engagement is trending downward. This decline is gaining momentum, at least according to the Pew Research Center which has been tracking these religious changes for some time.

In their publication, "Nones on the Rise,"[36] the overall conclusion is that "Nones" grew from 15% to 20% of the U.S. population in just 5 years. It is the demographic of those under 30, GenMe, where Pew found the largest decline: *over one third are unaffiliated with any religion.*[37] It is this slice of the population that the Pew study observes is responsible for almost all of the recent national religious decline. But, while this describes the religious state of the younger *adult* population, for those teens that I have worked with, the younger Millennials and the new Gen Z, the spiritual picture has more complex tones and tints.

MTD

Dr. Christian Smith of Notre Dame University conducted the largest and richest contemporary study of the religious lives of Millennials, tracking them from their teens into their twenties. Starting in 2002, Smith and his team began this unprecedented longitudinal inquiry funded by the Lilly Endowment, the National Study of Youth and Religion (NSYR).[38] In order to understand faith and other aspects of the lives of today's Millennials who were those teens, these insights are essential for elders to grasp. If anything, the situation has only become more challenging for the faith of youth today.

For the most part, the NSYR findings regarding American teens and emerging adults are clearly troubling to anyone who has studied them in detail. Here they are in brief which is all we need for now:

Most American teens in their study had some religious affiliation with 75% identifying themselves as Christians; 40% attending religious services weekly, prayed daily, and belonged to a youth group. Half said that their religion was important in their lives. *Not too bad.*

Most American teenagers studied have a positive view of religion—however, they also don't give it much thought; in their terms, it's not that big a deal. *This is troubling.*

Most U.S. teenagers mirror their parents' faith—while they are still mid-adolescents anyway. *Hopeful perhaps, but then it gets worse.*

Teenagers lack a sufficient language with which to express their faith or interpret their experience of the world in religious terms.

Supply and demand make a very large difference in their spiritual lives—where congregations, parents, and adults provide an array of religious opportunities for youth and make it a priority, they find positive life outcomes in teens. The reverse is also true and is far more common.

Only a very small minority (8%) of American teenagers are highly religious and express their faith as being very important to them and say it makes a difference in their daily lives. This is demonstrated by their doing significantly better on a range of life scales. This small cohort, approximately 1 in 12 teens, experience little or no change in their beliefs *after* high school. They sustain their faith and do not generally become Nones.

Religion does not take up much time or attention in the lives of American teenagers—it is viewed as an add-on, as optional when compared with other choices such as social networking, mass consumer capitalism, and expressive individualism.

Finally, this was the shocker that hit the religious community hard: many teenagers live and express their religious beliefs as something distinct from traditional religion—a world view dubbed Moralistic Therapeutic Deism (MTD), a term that has now entered the common vernacular.[39]

In essence, Smith concludes, most teens, (the 8% excluded) even though they attend church and often a youth group, exhibit a thin veneer of faith: MTD theology. These teenagers are "moralistic" in that they believe that God wants us to be good and that the main purpose of religion is to help people be good: "be nice and don't judge others." But since it is possible to be "good" without being religious, religion is an optional tool for them that can be chosen by those who find it helpful—or not—but it is not relevant for daily life. Obedience is also not emphasized. "Speaking the truth in love"[40] is now equivalent with "hate" or being judgmental.

American teen Christianity is also "therapeutic" Smith found, as many believe that God and religion are valuable to them, primarily because it helps them to feel better about their problems and most of all about themselves. Such therapeutic individualism is played out, for example, in the penchant for self-help books and programs that have vaguely religious contexts and language: the gospel according to Oprah and Dr. Phil.

Finally, American teenagers show their modern strain of "deism" by belief in a God who remains in the background of their lives—always watching over them, ready to help them, but not at the center of their lives in an ongoing relationship. A personal relationship with God is just not part of their language.

The NSYR summarizes their findings in what may be their most striking conclusion for elders and near elders:

> *A particular religious outlook that is distinct from the traditional faith commitments of most historical U.S. religious traditions, what we are calling Moralistic Therapeutic Deism, appears to have established a significant foothold among very many contemporary U.S. teenagers—When the engagement and education of American youth by their religious communities is weak, then the faith of teenagers in those traditions tends to degenerate into Moralistic Therapeutic Deism—actively displacing the substantive traditional faiths of conservative, black, and mainline Protestantism, Catholicism, and Judaism in the United States.*—It may be the new mainstream American religious faith for our culturally post-Christian, individualistic, mass-consumer, capitalist society (emphasis added).[41]

The "discovery" of this hidden (and, until recently, unnamed) world view over 15 years ago has made a deep impact on parents, pastors, youth workers, and theologians by raising their awareness of how things changed for the Millennial teens who are today's emerging adults now in their twenties and early thirties. This is where elders can benefit in understanding what has happened.

THE COLLEGE INQUISITION

The original cohort of Millennial high-schoolers was followed by Smith as they entered college then life beyond. The full impact of their *take it or leave it* beliefs is seen as these young adults underwent two great life transitions—high school to college; college to work life—normally in four or five years. These implications have only grown clearer with time.

Entering college and then the workforce, the younger generation is confronted with the more difficult changes, tests really, which shape them further as the cultivation of faith either continues or it wanes as they become older. This time of life serves much like the times of persecution in the early church or during the Inquisition—weak faith is exposed by the pressures of the dominant culture. The problems they face of intellectual skepticism and hostility along with the temptations of freedom (e.g., sex, alcohol, alternative lifestyles) reveal that the wheels that were wobbling in high school often come flying off as life accelerates and the culture around them is far more secular than they have experienced. Under such pressures, many walk away from the faith of their youth as they become emerging adults.

Emerging Adults

Experts who have studied this age group cite certain reasons not only for abandoning faith but for a newfound delay in reaching adulthood. These include a widespread growth in college and graduate school attendance which, in turn, is necessary for a knowledge economy; delays in marriage to almost a decade later than in the 1960s; a large rise in cohabitation and hooking up with fluid relationships becoming the norm; and a soft economic picture for many younger people. All these causes have had a hand in this younger generation's deferred adulthood/prolonged adolescence. We see this among 18-34 year-olds, who, for the first time in the modern era, are more often living with their parents than they are either married or cohabiting. Fully 35% of young men and 29% of young women are in these unprecedented living arrangements. As recently as 1960, the year I entered college, fully 56% of the men in this same age group and 68% of the women were either married or cohabiting (the vast majority were married).[42]

39

What Smith found is going on in the lives of the decade of those from their late teens to their late twenties is troubling to elders. Rather than seeking to settle down there is instead an "intense identity exploration, instability, a focus on self, feeling in limbo or in transition or in between, and a sense of possibilities, opportunities, and unparalleled hope—accompanied by large doses of transience, confusion, anxiety, self-obsession, melodrama, conflict, disappointment, and sometimes emotional devastation."[43] Think *Seinfeld* or *Friends* as the gentler depiction of what Smith describes.

With the transition to responsible adulthood now delayed almost ten years from what was the norm fifty years ago, has come a generational culture characterized by shallow moral roots. For most, Smith found, it is a time of life that evidences a marked rise in consumerism; excessive use of alcohol and drugs; casual sex; and civic and political disengagement.[44]

The good news, if there is some, is that for those relatively few teens whose faith was integral to their lives, the NSYR found, overwhelmingly, they did sustain that faith into college and beyond. There is hope in that insight.

Thus, the "decline" in religious practice seen among emerging adults in college and beyond is perhaps not so puzzling after all. In reality, the vigor of faith in the teen years that was most often expressed in outward compliance but inward indifference, *acedia*, is a harbinger of the rise of the Nones. Disengagement of hearts began well before college and most could not stand up to the hurricane of modern secular distractions. For some, their hearts were likely never changed in the first place. Accompanying the failure of faith to mature in the modern world is a delay in other aspects of adulthood.

While this understanding is a very important context for us elders to grasp, as this story unfolds don't lose hold of the thread that it is the older generations who shape the younger generations. We are simply describing symptoms seen in many of those who are younger right now, not fully diagnosing causes just yet. There remains one more indictor to further understand before we can explore the root cause and how elders can best be of help.

OH, MISERY

Being raised in the 50s meant I was among the first teen generation in which music was written explicitly for us. It spoke to where we were, with a beat of course. One such singer/songwriter was Buddy Holly out of Lubbock, Texas, whose tragic early death in an airplane crash shocked the nation. For my generation, what we found to be most painful was love—found and lost—as Holly gives voice to it in *It's Raining in My Heart*.

> *The sun is out, the sky is blue*
> *There's not a cloud to spoil the view*
> *But it's raining, raining in my heart*
> *The weather man says clear today*
> *He doesn't know you've gone away*
> *And it's raining, raining in my heart*
> *Oh, misery, misery*
> *What's gonna become of me?*[45]

Now, it's easy to make fun of my teenage self and my friends, being so woeful when "my baby" broke up with me. But the misery of the Millennials and Generation Z may not be looked back upon with such a knowing adult chuckle: these young people are often deeply stressed! It shows up in a significant increase in anxiety, depression, and, God help us, suicide, which are now all at unprecedented levels.

21 Pilots (Fueled by Ramen) capture the angst of this time for the young in *Stressed Out*, part of the largest selling digital album in history with every song going Gold or Platinum:

> *I was told when I get older all my fears would shrink*
> *But now I'm insecure and I care what people think*

41

Wish we could turn back time, to the good old days...
When our momma sang us to sleep but now we're stressed out
We're stressed out

Sometimes a certain smell will take me back to when I was young
How come I'm never able to identify where it's coming from
I'd make a candle out of it if I ever found it...
But it would remind us of when nothing really mattered
Out of student loans and tree-house homes we all would take the latter...

We used to play pretend, give each other different names
We would build a rocket ship and then we'd fly it far away
Used to dream of outer space but now they're laughing at our face

Saying, "Wake up, you need to make money"... [46]

Take for example that the *average* college student in the 1990s was more anxious than 85% of the college students in the 1950s and that *normal* schoolchildren in the 1980s would have been child psychiatric patients 30 years earlier using the same measures.[47] This trend worsened in the 2000s with severe increases in depression, anxiety, unrealistic self-appraisal, over-activity, and low self-control. In just 30 years, high school students reporting depression and anxiety have also had a threefold increase in insomnia and a doubling of those seeing a doctor for mental health issues. [48] These are not just statistics, these are the young among us—this alarm is not the boy crying wolf.

I have counseled both high schoolers and those now in college and, almost to a person, they have told me they have experienced anxiety, a few with thoughts of suicide—and these are young adults whose faith is otherwise solid. That experience extends to the older emerging adults whom I have talked with who are out of college and well into their twenties. Many are seeing a therapist or taking anti-depressants or are on anti-anxiety medication and feeling stressed, lonely, confused about relationships or vocational choices, and questioning their futures.

As people have begun to study the new iGen, the picture darkens even more. When Dr. Jean Twenge, who pioneered work on the Millennials, began to see sharp changes in teen behavior and mood around 2012, she did not know what to make of it. Teens were spending far less time with friends, they were much lonelier, and anxiety and depression were far worse, if possible. With all of this, it is no wonder she found they also feel far less safe than those who preceded them. To be sure, some apparently good results were also appearing—teens were less likely to have sex and dating was declining as was the age of first driving. Still, this was perplexing for her.[49] Her conclusion: as the title suggests, what began to happen by 2012 was that with widely available smartphones came more misery in their wake. Maybe. It certainly is a big part of the picture and deserves to be clearly understood with the first members of this generation still in college, the long-term situation is yet unclear. Undoubtedly, the level of angst among so many Millennials has only gotten worse as the next generation has taken their place in line.

Miserable? Pretty much, certainly by all known historical standards. Millennials and now the iGen not only have been eating the thin gruel of their self-centered religion, they have grown weak in the deep places of their hearts and souls and the symptoms have been identified for our deeper understanding and response. Still, there is more to this story than simply younger generations in great need while elders shake their heads.

THE PIVOT

As I write this, seeking to transition our conversation to the older generations, I am reminded of the beginning of Paul's magisterial letter to the Romans. Paradoxically, the way he begins this momentous letter leads me to chuckle every time I read it—primarily at myself. He starts out by listing all the ways the Gentiles are going downhill—spiritually, morally, socially, sort of like the Millennials and Gen Z. He gets his Jewish readers' heads shaking

43

in agreement as our gray ones might as we review the ills of these "kids." In reading this maybe you are tempted to think of "them" and what a mess they are making of their lives. But Paul makes that surprising pivot as he turns to the next part of his letter addressing his Jewish readers:

> *Therefore you have no excuse, O man, every one of you who judges. For in passing judgment on another you condemn yourself, because you, the judge, practice the very same things. We know that the judgment of God rightly falls on those who practice such things. Do you suppose, O man—you who judge those who practice such things and yet do them yourself—that you will escape the judgment of God?[50]*

Whew! If we use Paul's framework in addressing these two major groups, Jew and Gentile, it might cause us to think more soberly together about our age. If so, join me in realizing that the Millennials did not simply parachute into our midst looking for a soft place to land while they check their phones. They are the product of our culture, of their elders, an era of advancing individualism and of the ever-growing orthodoxy of secular relativism. And, yes, they are taking longer to grow up and assume the responsibilities that their elders (we) did at far younger ages. But built into the DNA of creation and the advancement of God's kingdom is this simple truth: one generation, for good or for ill, teaches the next. It has to, whether consciously or not.

While we may be tempted to think that both the root cause and the solution lies in the Millennials and Gen Z getting off their phones and getting their immature acts together, I'd suggest those who are older need to dig deeper and go further up and farther in. A look back at our formation might give us a better understanding of what lies at the root of today's generational challenges: as we were shaped, so we arrived today at the future.

Here is one passage in Psalm 78 you might reflect upon that nailed me as I thought more deeply about all of this:

We will not hide them from their children, but tell to the coming generation the glorious deeds of the LORD, and his might, and the wonders that he has done. He established a testimony in Jacob and appointed a law in Israel, which he commanded our fathers to teach to their children, that the next generation might know them, the children yet unborn, and arise and tell them to their children, so that they should set their hope in God and not forget the works of God, but keep his commandments; and that they should not be like their fathers, a stubborn and rebellious generation, a generation whose heart was not steadfast, whose spirit was not faithful to God. [51]

How's that going for us? The young *are* a weak link right now and we might rightly be concerned for *their* children, but the Bible encourages us not to look at things analytically, fragmented, in isolation from the context. We also need to see why elders are a weakened link, too. We are the connecting link in the chain that goes back to the apostles and further. My generation was brought up in the so-called good life of *Father Knows Best's* benign home rule or *Amos and Andy's* comforting black ineptitude; by the Kennedys' altruistic vision and their untimely deaths; and by Martin Luther King's oration and persistence to his tragic end; by Vietnam and by The Pill; by *duck-and-cover* and by Elvis. The good old days may bring nostalgia, but they weren't all that good, either. We need to understand ourselves then as elders through the lens of the Kierkegaard paradox, whether we are among the Veteran Generation, the Boomers, or Gen X. Understanding how we were formed matters to us today—that is if we are to take up our intended roles at the gate.

CHAPTER 4

WHO TRAINED THE CANARIES TO SING?

We are now—in the Me Decade—seeing the upward roll (and not yet the crest, by any means) of the third great religious wave in American history, one that historians will very likely term the Third Great Awakening. Like the others it has begun in a flood of ecstasy, achieved through LSD and other psychedelics, orgy, dancing (the New Sufi and the Hare Krishna), meditation, and psychic frenzy (the marathon encounter)...[52]

What if these "kids" we've been talking about are the canaries in our 21st Century coal mine, warning those of us who came of age in the 50s or 60s or 70s of impending danger? It is not unreasonable that they sense the toxic fumes of our culture—an early warning for us of an urgent if yet undetected need right in front of our noses.

Whether we were consciously aware of it or not, we elders were the ones who trained them to "sing," and the silencing of their joy may be a portentous warning. They were not born with MTD implanted in their cell structure; anxiety and individualism were not passed on in their DNA; there was not a convention Boomers called to decide that the coming generations would be slow to mature.

They came by it all honestly while we elders were a bit younger ourselves, still trying to figure it all out. The task at hand for elders is to become humble enough to learn to turn around and serve those coming behind; to own up to our responsibilities to them today while recognizing how we were shaped in our youth.

Let's take the rise of the Nones as an example. The case can be made that it is simply the denouement of what many have warned of for some time—Christianity in the United States and in the West has been becoming only tenuously Christian. If the faith of the young has substantially morphed into Christianity's misbegotten MTD step-cousin, *it is not just the young that evidence this; they had to learn it from us somehow.* This certainly began happening among many individual believers within the church and inside the structures of many of the Christian organizations and institutions dating back at least to the late 19th century.

Many, for example, saw the harbingers of demise in the culling of biblical language: holiness, blood, sin, grace, justification, sanctification, celibacy, suffering, Sabbath, and Hell. We are now apt to hear the more accommodating terms such as happiness, niceness, inclusion, "judge not," and heavenly reward for us all—at least in many quarters. It is not so much that Western Christianity is being secularized, though it has been. Rather, more subtly, many see Christianity as either degenerating into an edited version of itself, or, more significantly, Christianity is actively being colonized and displaced by a quite different religious faith altogether.[53] As elders, it began (or perhaps picked up speed) in *our* youth, but it threatens our successors even more in these latter years of their coming of age. We have unwittingly spawned MTD in ways I've only lately come to realize myself.

Juvenilization Began Here

Ironically, perhaps, there is some evidence that it was the enormous past success of youth ministry that many of us knew back in its heyday in the 50s and 60s that has contributed to the more recent decline in spiritual maturity in our young today. The lessons drawn from the post-World War II rise of para-church youth ministries such as Young Life, Youth for Christ, Campus Crusade for

Christ (now Cru), and Youth with a Mission, that nurtured many who are older, began to be implemented on a wider scale by the church as a whole. "By the time the 1960s counterculture hit the mainstream, the [evangelical] youth movement was well-practiced in adapting its messages and methods to young people (as a type of counterculture itself). Mainline churches bled youth membership; evangelical affiliation boomed."[54] But it was this very numerical success that led to the methods being copied by many churches in both mainline and evangelical camps in their efforts to grow in the wake of the movement that put the Jesus Revolution on the cover of *Time* magazine. These adaptations in the church to open their worship format to seekers and the young led to what Thomas E. Bergler names as "the juvenilization of American Christianity."[55]

He traces these roots as beginning even before World War II, when churches experimented with how to better reach young people in the midst of the Great Depression and before the horrors of World War II. Many at the time feared a "lost generation" in the crises that ran unabated for years. What emerged after the war was the first categorization of "teenager" and the phenomenon that Bergler says continues to this day—the desire of many of the now not-so-young to remain youthful with all that portends.[56] In case you missed it, he's talking about those who are now the elders.

The final step in the process he says was *the transformation of American adulthood* itself. Older cultural conceptions of adulthood encouraged responsibility, self-denial, and service to others. In the first half of the 20th century, most people clearly entered adulthood in their teens or early 20s by virtue of getting married, getting a job, and having children. More recently, as we discussed earlier, the passage to adulthood has been delayed and rendered more subjective—yet it didn't just begin with the Millennials.

In what sociologist James Cote calls the new "psychological adulthood," the individual's "needs and wants" expanded and his or her "obligations and attachments" contracted. The seven deadly sins have been redefined, he says: "pride has become self-esteem;

49

lust has become sexuality; envy is now channeled into initiative and incentive; sloth has become leisure."[57] Of course, many adults still value virtue and deplore vice, but as a whole the plausibility structure of American culture—what most people believe is true about maturity—has become a view of life as an unending journey of self-development and discovery. Whether Veterans, Boomers, or Gen Xers, this cultural trend is evident in the choices people make and the opportunities that are generated for this growing market.

Thus, the contemporary landscape through which the elders journeyed as they grew older has had many paths that pointed toward the self-centeredness or narcissism of lasting youth. In short, some traits evidenced as ripe fruit in Christian maturity have been slowly detached from adulthood beginning at least in post-1960's America if not before. This change has in turn also encouraged the juvenilization of theology. Indeed, the relative immaturity of some forms of American Christianity and the parallel emergence of the new trends in adulthood have mutually reinforced one another. We're all adolescents now to some extent.[58]

What Bergler observed at work within the Catholic and Protestant churches in the mid-twentieth century has, in his analysis, emerged in the form of the twenty-first century MTD in the young. Good intentions based on wrong conclusions have produced unintended consequences. Juvenilization tends to create a self-centered, emotionally driven, and intellectually/spiritually empty faith and sadly it seems to have been transmitted from one generation to another like an altered gene. For example, the phrase "feel happy," which strikingly appeared over 2,000 times in 267 interviews by the NSYR, is much akin to the world view Boomer parents and grandparents became known for.

Today, many religious Americans of all ages accept a Christianized version of adolescent narcissism, and often celebrate it as "authentic" spirituality. *God, faith, and the church all exist to help me with my problems.* We go to church for therapy. Teenagers learn these altered beliefs from the adults in their lives as well as from the ubiquitous media.

The emergence of the shallow MTD theology that may shock or appall us today has been a long time in the making it seems. Like many theological trends, it started with some good goals, but in its evolution and in the further shaping of it by the changing culture, modern theology became distorted into what the NSYR uncovered as being unique to our youth. It's not. Popular culture more than the Bible is ascendant. As elders, we tend to forget that before there was a GenMe there was a Me Generation—a Me Decade even—long before the Millennials were a glint in a sociologist's eye. Some self-reflection might be in order.

The Me Decade

Tom Wolfe may have had his finger on the American pulse better than almost any writer of our era. He was the first to offer a brilliant summary of the cultural emergence that shook America in the 60s and came to fruition in the 70s, dubbing it the Me Decade. He likened it to nothing less than the Third Great Awakening as he saw in its fervor something almost religious though thoroughly secular. His literary technique was to have his readers just listen in on Boomers' conversations as a way to understand how different the world was becoming:

> *They begin with… "Let's talk about Me." They begin with the most delicious look inward; with considerable narcissism, in short. When the believers bind together into religions, it is always with a sense of splitting off from the rest of society. We, the enlightened (lit by the sparks at the apexes of our souls), hereby separate ourselves from the lost souls around us. Like all religions before them, they proselytize—but always on promising the opposite of nationalism: a City of Light that is above it all. There is no ecumenical spirit within this Third Great Awakening. If anything, there is a spirit of schism.[59]*

This vast wave of post-World War II babies, coming of age in the 60s and 70s were pioneers of self-focus and perhaps nothing captured their yearning better than the runaway best seller of the day *Jonathan Livingston Seagull*, the story of the bird who dared to be different. Rather than engage in the raucous, boring hunt for food like the rest of the flock, Jonathan preferred to live his life soaring above it all, using his gifts to fly rather than engage in tendentious fights over a dead fish. This was what it was to be young in the 60's.

The desire to be free of the crowd manifested itself in the perplexity of their elders. The staple joke in sitcoms of the era was the conflict between a young person "finding themselves" and an elder mumbling something about "why not find a job, instead?" Think Archie Bunker and his son-in-law, "Meathead."

Jean Twenge in her research on today's Millennials says to understand them you first need to understand the Boomers because they practically invented narcissism, though it has morphed into something far more intensive in their grandchildren. In other words, if you are an elder, you need to humbly examine your own roots first.

For one, Boomers were intent upon the inner journey of self-discovery, of knowing themselves, of finding purpose and meaning in life. Theirs was a time when *spirituality* was intensely sought, whether in the awakening of the Jesus Movement or in the wisdom of a guru, typified by the Beatles' own Maharishi Mahesh Yogi. The spiritual journey was often enhanced by hallucinogens such as LSD, peyote, and of course marijuana. Songwriters praised the wonders opened up by drugs, e.g., The Dawning of the Age of Aquarius. "Pot" or "weed" has now been mainstreamed.

By the late 60s, almost 7 out of 8 incoming college freshmen said their goal was to develop a meaningful philosophy of life[60] and many expressed their deep interest in changing the world as they launched group movements and protests of the establishment. Ironically for our day's youth, this belief of the Boomers included faith in government to make change (e.g., the Peace Corps), all before Nixon's Watergate sullied public service. They rallied to the challenge: "Ask not what your country can do for you. Ask what you can do for your country!"

FREEDOM FOR SEX

And then there was the advent of the birth control pill in 1960 which freed women from what some felt was oppression and launched the free love movement with implications that continue to flow through the culture. A loss of consequences and the emergence of female equality in sexuality opened the doors to today's hook-up culture. It was in the 60s that the Centers for Disease Control began to note a precipitous decline in the bonds of marriage and a rising wave of STDs. Divorce rates began pushing upward from 22% in 1960 to over 50% for first marriages.[61] No-fault divorce became a nationwide legal initiative beginning in 1969—in California under the divorced Governor Ronald Reagan.[62]

Marriage today has become slightly more stable than it was at the very height of the rising divorce rates in the 1970s, falling to around 40% for first time marriages, but this is mainly due to far later marriages and to the now common cohabitation practice and hookup culture. Unfortunately, this slight decline has been socially disproportional: divorce rates among the non-college educated have actually risen while among the college educated it has declined.[63]

Overall the changing cultural values in the very meaning of marriage or even the need for marriage is what characterizes our age with Europe setting the pace. None of this is good for the younger generations' relationships. Today's Millennials are far more wary of covenantal or contractual bonds, often being the products of the high divorce rate of previous generations. Thus, the pleasures of travel and consumption and being happy coupled with delayed responsibility is where they seek to find their fulfillment well into their 30s.

Unlike Boomers, Millennials believe it is also more important to feel good about yourself than to have a philosophy of life or to change the order of things in the world, especially through government.

The Boomers certainly had ambition, not only to change the world, but also to eat the fruits of their labors in ever more upscale ways. David Brooks describes their attitudes toward materialism as they aged:

> *I found that if you investigated people's attitudes toward sex, morality, leisure time, and work, it was getting harder and harder to separate the anti-establishment renegade from the pro-establishment company man. Most people, at least among the college-educated set, seemed to have rebel attitudes and social-climbing attitudes all scrambled together. Defying expectations and maybe logic, people seemed to have combined the countercultural sixties and the achieving eighties into one social ethos.[64]*

This was the soil in which the younger generations grew. But the most potent impact came courtesy of something few that do not work with youth are even aware of.

ABANDONMENT

Briefly tracing the extensive change which has occurred within the lifetime of those who are now elders can help clarify the extent to which the older generations have contributed to the results seen now in the late to mature younger generations. We elders shaped today's youth and emerging adults. The major changes however are not limited to shifts in theology, the rise of expressive individualism, the liberation of sexuality, or the materialistic lifestyles. There is still something missing we need to understand as to why the bonds between generations have become strained by us elders, not just by the youth. There's one more contributing factor that has flown under the radar and this is very crucial for us to grasp, for it has serious implications for the vocation of elders.

Chap Clark, the Vice Provost and Professor of Youth, Family, and Culture at Fuller Theological Seminary, and the head of their Institute of Youth Ministry has conducted extensive research on American youth spanning more than a decade. His questions focus on understanding the formation of youth into spiritually mature adults in the midst of these major cultural shifts in America after World War II. His conclusions begin with a telling observation for those of us who are elders at the gate—as well as for the church and for parents:

> *Those who control and define the systems and structures charged with nurturing and training up our young (and especially those who have the power associated with them) are either ignorant of how destructive life is for today's adolescents or unwilling to take the wide array of indicators seriously.*[65]

"Destructive" is a strong word for the leading role of elders in the lives of today's young, but he has good reason to arrive there. He points out that in our current culture, it is to the *institutions* in society that today's parents turn most often to nurture their young. He has found that this modern solution to forming youth (at least in the West) whether it is in music, sports, or education—even in faith—has had poor if unintended consequences.

In part, he says this nurturing shift toward relying on the expertise of institutions has occurred out of the depth and breadth of the cultural changes of the past forty years. These have left adults busier, more stressed, and increasingly isolated even as home sizes and commuting times have grown and the internet has transformed home life more than TV ever did. The resulting outcome of relying far more on institutions to form our youth, he says, has devastated the social capital (particularly the adult-youth personal interactions) that are essential to forming adolescents into adults. He sees this shift over the last decades as the primary reason why the young are losing their faith, delaying maturity, and finding themselves far more anxious and depressed. He traces a stark downward path leading to these results:

As society in general moved from being a relatively stable and cohesive adult community intent on caring for the needs of the young to a free-for-all of independent and fragmented adults seeking their own survival, individual adolescents found themselves in a deepening hole of systemic rejection. This rejection, or abandonment, of adolescents is the root of the fragmentation and calloused distancing that are the hallmarks of the adolescent culture.[66] (emphasis added)

"Abandonment," "rejection:" these are more harsh words to hear. They have the tone of willfulness, suggesting a conscious, callous choice by selfish people. It also smacks of finger pointing and it points uncomfortably to us if we are older. My first reaction when I saw this research was to push back. Since then, I've thought about it more and read more widely. Yes, it is not quite that simple perhaps, but the implications are critical for us elders to understand, for if he is right in what he has uncovered, we have work to do. And it is good work.

The ongoing research by Fuller Youth Institute and Clark has only grown more confident in their primary conclusion: *"abandonment" is the defining issue for contemporary adolescents and for those now in their twenties.*[67] It is probably the tap root of the issues the younger generations are experiencing. Let's see why.

Forming in Maturity

The key formative period for adults is between 15 and 19 years of age—where the life experiences from the sophomore year in high school to the freshman year in college exert the most leverage on who they are becoming—the formation of character and mental habits. It is the time when the latest neuroscience research tells us the critical last phase of brain development is simultaneously occurring. The depth of relationships with adults—parents and others—in forming secure, safe personal attachments is the central activity in the proper maturing of the brain during this time.[68]

56

The issue of abandonment, unintentional adult neglect, in some ways puts a different spin on what we have known for many years: the lack of face time with children is a growing phenomenon of our time. In the public discussions of what is happening to the young, it is not something most of us would readily connect with the issues of formation we have been outlining here. What was not appreciated by most observers was that the consequence of what was earlier identified as rising therapeutic and expressive individualism among adults as early as the early 1970s and 1980s—a devotion to focusing on and feeling good about ourselves—is now seen as having played out in spades in how today's adolescents and emerging adults have been shaped. It seems that just as adults began to turn inward (and their lives became far busier[69]) the needs of the young were growing hungrier for individual engagement with older, wiser people, even though they could not articulate this desire. Instead that loss was communicated by the symptoms the "canaries" have been evidencing—the singing has stopped. That the old and the young alike have also begun to live with screen addiction[70] from the advent of TV in the late 60s to today's ever-present smart phones has only enhanced the unlinking of our natural relationships and attachments. The outcomes are far more portentous than when individualism was first raised as the mark of postmodern culture.[71]

Most academics and adults in the professions responsible for nurturing youth now hold to what Chap Clark and Fuller Youth Institute concluded: "*Adolescents need adults to become adults, and when adults are not present in their lives, they are forced to figure out how to survive life on their own.*"[72]

Going further, Clark and his colleagues also found that in response "the way mid-adolescents have been forced to design their own world and invent a separate social system has created perhaps the most serious and yet understudied social crisis of our time."[73]

Abandonment in some form began to be recognized as early as the 1980s when David Elkind's, *The Hurried Child,* appeared.[74] The

57

characteristic he described as "hurry" became the "abandonment" Clark outlines three decades later in the highly programmed lives of many adolescents:

> *By the time adolescents enter high school, nearly everyone has been subjected to a decade or more of adult-driven and adult-controlled programs, systems, and institutions that are primarily concerned with adults' agendas, needs, and dreams... We have evolved to the point where we believe driving is support, being active is love, and providing any and every opportunity is selfless nurture. We are a culture that has forgotten how to be together. We have lost the ability to spend unstructured down time... We as a culture have looked to outside organizations and structured agendas to fill their time and dictate their lives. The problem is not simply organized activities or sports. It is the cumulative effect that children experience as they grow up in today's social structure. Sports, music, dance, drama, Scouts, and even faith-related programs are all guilty of ignoring the developmental needs of each individual young person in favor of the organization's goals. Add to this the increasing amount of homework being assigned to students at younger and younger ages. The systemic pressure on American children is immense."[75]*

Clark says "more subtle yet far more insidious" is the lost place for safety and intimacy that used to exist down through time.

The postmodern family is often so concerned about the needs, struggles, and issues of parents that the emotional and developmental needs of the children go largely unmet. Add to this trend the rarity of the extended family available to the vast majority of adolescents, the deemphasizing of the importance of marriage, and the lack of healthy relationships with adults as friends and mentors, and it is easy to see why today's adolescent faces an internal crisis of unprecedented scope."[76]

Perhaps the simplest way to summarize is this. For many the

mid-adolescent experience has been that no adults were really there for them within the normal course of a day. In response, they developed their own social capital and relationship systems with their own rules that lay beneath the surface of detection typically used by surveys and studies involving observation and self-reporting.

No longer do teens form social cliques, but rather Clark's team discovered the existence of "clusters" of support among peers.[77] As Patricia Hersh has aptly put it, they have become "a tribe apart."[78] Go down to any urban gathering spot for 20- and 30-somethings—bars and coffee houses in particular—and you will see it lived out in small groups, "hanging out" as they are prone to say, which is simply an extension of what began in high school.

If we add to this the ubiquity of divorce, family conflicts, and one-parent families, you have a recipe for the crisis that transcends the issue of faith formation in an MTD world as it plays out more widely in a general failure in our culture of maturing at the age when earlier generations did so. Understanding the role of adult abandonment, I believe, is the critical component for our purposes here in framing why elders have an irreplaceable responsibility for the spiritual and adult formation of youth and emerging adults, and that role is critical.

What all this leads to underscores two things we have already observed. First, the unprecedented delay in taking on the role of adults where so many remain in a semi-frozen state of late adolescence even with professional work responsibilities. Second, the sense younger people have of loneliness, anxiety, and depression on their maturing journey is for good reason and this "hurts" them more than we have realized.[79] For many teens and for those entering the next stage of life in college and after graduation, not even God is present. Where once God may have been at least a remote presence, now he seems AWOL to them at the critical junctures they face. My friend Anne who works with young people in their twenties in Washington D.C. sees this loss of connection and loneliness all the time and it is grievous—but it is certainly not hopeless by any means. It's a challenge, a good one, we who are elder can take on one by one.

Let us understand then, becoming an adult in this generation is likely far more difficult than for any generation before on earth. In fact, one of the more humorous results has been the change in language noted earlier in the use of "to adult" and its gerund, "adulting" to describe responsible behavior. Merriam Webster reports that "the first five months of 2016 saw a six-fold increase in the use of these terms."[80] When my granddaughter first used it to describe doing the laundry, I knew the apocalypse was upon us.

More seriously, the support systems previously provided by parents and other adults have become far weaker, while the negative cultural and theological influences have become much stronger. It is no wonder the symptoms of anxiety and depression and narcissism have soared, maturity is prolonged, and solid faith becomes rarer.

What is important at this point in our story is to move beyond simply understanding the nature of the weaknesses in each link—elder with younger—whether to decry what we elders did in our earlier years to contribute to weakening the links or to wring our hands over today's younger generations. We who are elders need to prepare to make better choices now in these last years we are given by grace. For me, the best way to do this has been to discover that mentoring was built into our design as human beings, not only as a responsibility, but one for which we are actually well equipped to carry out if we have eyes to see. Nowhere is this more clearly explained than in the ancient scriptures of Judaism and Christianity. It is a wonder I missed this all these years. Perhaps you have as well.

Chapter 5

Mentors Are MIA

Train up a child in the way he should go; even when he is old he will not depart from it.[81]

Moses is likely one of the single most amazing leaders the world has ever known, yet one of its most underappreciated. How does someone lead a ragtag group of over two million poorly armed slaves through 40 years of living as nomads and refugees in a desert wilderness? How are they prepared then, after all that, to conquer a land which had great wealth and several armies equipped well beyond anything the Hebrews could muster? How does he govern such a vast number of wandering people or provide for their physical needs? Yet, history shows that is exactly what happened.

So it was at the end of those forty long years of the peripatetic, senseless-seeming journey from Egypt, just before they enter the Promised Land, Moses gives the people his final instructions, likely shouted from rank to rank of the multitudes of people. He knew his part of the journey was about to end just short of the goal. Thus, in his final address he stresses the importance of keeping all of the statutes that the Lord had given them. He admonished the younger generations to remember the dependability of the Lord's provision over the decades, but also to keep in mind his discipline which fell on their elders for lack of faith. As their now grown children, he wanted to ensure that *their* faith in God would be sustained down through the next generations: "Only take care and keep your soul diligently, lest you forget the things that your eyes have seen, and lest they depart from your heart all the days of your life. *Make them known to your children and to your children's children.*"[82] Then, Moses repeats the Ten Commandments and concludes with the Shema, the Great Commandment. In my imagination, this was delivered Charlton Heston-like in ringing, never-to-be-forgotten tones to the Jewish people he loved and had given his elder years to:

> *Hear O Israel, The LORD our God, the LORD is one. You shall love the LORD you God with all your heart and with all your soul, and with all your might. And these words that I command you this day shall be upon your heart. You shall teach them diligently to your children, and shall talk of them when you sit in your house, and when you walk by the way, and when you lie down, and when you rise.*[83]

Underscoring the importance of this principle, God, speaking through Moses, repeats the very same admonition twice, then a third time in Chapter 11 of Deuteronomy. Three times for emphasis—don't miss the point. Perhaps more recognizable for Christians, this was precisely what Jesus responded when asked about the greatest of all of Moses' commandments with the common supposition that his hearers would know the entire context of the commandment. One generation was to teach the next about rightly ordered love of God and of neighbor. To obey God and to trust him out of deep love and remembrance of what he has done—all of this is grist for the regular teaching of and modeling for children and emerging adults in our day.

This intergenerational practice was to be a natural part of all of life whether in the house, out in the fields, or working under the car together; whether going to bed or at the first light of day; at a coffee shop, on the trail, or at the dinner table—the love of God and obedience to his commandments is passed on by example, by apprenticeship, by story, and by teaching. It is first the task of parents, then of all adults who are within the community, begun by those who crossed the Red Sea and survived the wilderness journey then by those coming afterward down across the centuries to ours as but the latest. It is the first task of each succeeding generation of adults in the community of those who follow God: to teach the love of God and of others in living life under the sun. This responsibility was not to be abandoned, but I'm afraid we have let that thread slip through our fingers, as did they.

Solomon picks up on this in Proverbs 22 as almost 400 years later it became the recorded wisdom of the community: "Train up a child in the way he should go and when he is old he will not depart from it."[84] He reiterates the principle that the formation of a follower of God must begin in their youth so that when they become adults they will not "drop out" and follow other gods or other allurements. This admonition was important because by the era when David's son ruled, many mistakes had already been made by Israel in following that important teaching. Ironically, Solomon himself had failed at just that point with his own son; and David himself did as well.

If there is any fundamental principle of scripture that has seemingly been violated or at least ignored down through the years this is it. While the church and the older generations may decry what they see in today's American youth, the clear scriptural responsibility for what we see lies with parents and other adults in the spiritual community. The lost methods God prescribes could be described as life-apprenticing relationships. In their place it seems institutions have taken the place of these formational relationships.

To be sure, my intent in this book is not a jeremiad. There are still many places where youth are well formed for the long run by adults. My wife and I know many of them in our church community who are spiritually and personally far more mature than we were at their age. There are also many people who do take the time and assume the responsibility to walk alongside the younger generation consistently and authentically—living, teaching, and apprenticing gospel living and you will hear some of their stories. It is the *community*, not the religious institution or the church programs *per se* that is the key to taking up our adult-forming responsibilities given to us. Yet, for most of the last few decades, it is youth and young adult ministries in churches that have borne the weight to spiritually form younger Christians—not their parents or adult friends and mentors in an intergenerational community of worship.

If we are to understand then how to take up the question of how wisdom is to be better formed in those younger, we must go beyond defining the problems of the connecting generational links and begin to see what elders might do by looking first at the church itself, the richest culture within which to see mentoring grow.

Chapter 6

The Culture for Growing Mentors

I think if this whole mentoring thing got off the ground we would change the church in America; we would change education in America... We would have a tremendous impact on the quality of our families. If there is one thing the devil wants to do it's destroy the family because after that it's not a problem. I think mentoring is one of the possibilities for us to reverse those things.[85]

Mentoring is an intergenerational activity. For most when they hear *mentor* they naturally think about the workplace where mentoring is often used as a way to inculcate new hires into the ways of the organization or to develop managers and leaders. That may even have been your experience. However, our conversation involves those looking toward becoming or who already are elders, most of whom have left or will leave the workplace behind. Most churches are fully intergenerational from babies to nonagenarians and are the natural soil for all we have discussed and will ahead.

Most often, churches and parents alike look primarily to youth and young adult ministries as the institutions responsible for forming children, teens, and emerging adults whether they are church-based or parachurch organizations that specialize in certain demographics. For example, parents of teens who are concerned about their children's faith, finding a church with an active youth ministry is a top priority. Absent that, a group like Young Life or

Focus is essential for the task at hand. For those who are emerging adults in college and afterward into their 30s, an active singles ministry is often their desired find. Certainly, such vibrant ministries can be and often are a key component in spiritual and life formation. But, as the loss of faith among the young has become more evident, there has been some recent rethinking of such ministries. There are far brighter and more experienced people working in this field than me and our purpose here is not to be sidetracked from understanding the role of elders purposed for them to take up in the last part of life. Rather, in understanding where new ideas in youth and emerging adult ministry are heading, you might well see a role you can play within your church as the best place to start. I'll also offer the church I am best familiar with, my own, as a place seeking to better do what we are discussing.

A Benchmark

One example I found in trying to better understand the younger folks I have been working with comes from the approach summarized in the Exemplary Youth Ministry Study. It gives us at least two clues that are helpful for our inquiry about the role of elders and our reaching back to the next generation.

The Exemplary Youth Ministry Study identified "best practices," benchmarks which most often produced a sustained, unshaken faith in young people, not the sham form, MTD. What the researchers found as normative in those churches that did it best was they seriously invest in their youth and it is not ancillary. They have a full-time youth minister with a variety of opportunities for youth but *heavily engaged in by many other adults*. They involve the younger members in acts of service and in the experience of real leadership and responsibility as part of the community, not simply in "fun" activities designed to draw high participation. These best practices youth ministries also possess at least the following characteristics which combine (1 sound and mature theology; (2 multiple opportunities:

- They portray God as living, present, and active with whom we are meant to live in relationship
- A high value is placed on the importance of scripture publicly and in private
- The mission, relationships, and practices of the church (or organization) are understood to be grounded in Jesus Christ—his mission for his followers and his transforming power to carry it out
- They emphasize spiritual growth and maturity, discipleship, and vocation for each person for all of life as normative and progressive
- They have an outward focus of outreach and mission rather than in inward focus on building numbers or providing entertainment
- They help cultivate in the young a spirit of a secure hope for the future and lives of moral seriousness and service as younger adults.[86]

The takeaway is two-pronged: many adults are necessarily engaged in the ministry in some form, not just the youth minister and a couple of helpers. Here we see that to impact younger people, *relationships are key*. The lone ranger, charismatic youth leader is not where it's at today.

Real life models who are older *teach* what a mature faith looks like when it is walking around in the body of caring adults who give time to those younger. Given all we have discussed thus far, these churches can be seen as life-giving islands within a vast ocean of Gen Z and Millennial need. If you are an elder, here may be a place for you where you are badly needed, regardless of your age, that is if your church has such an approach. If you are a pastor or youth worker, I'd recommend checking this out and maybe talking with churches that are using adults in this way.

One place is my own church, Restoration Anglican in Arlington, Virginia. When we began as a church plant in 2010 there were probably around 70 people, mostly younger couples and singles, worshiping in an old Baptist church we acquired. Now there are over 700 with a healthy mix of all ages. Along the way, young kids grew up and were added and became teens. One of our first hires was Isaiah Brooms. Here is how he tells his story:

> *I spent my early childhood years living in an inner-city Chicago housing project called Cabrini Green. Born with an appetite for academics, a positive outlook on life (even in my rough situation) and a strong belief that God was in control, my high school years saw me elevated from those circumstances and thriving at an elite boarding school. As I continued to experience success, access, and achievements, I was blessed to be surrounded by individuals who not only kept me humble, but reminded me time and time again of the importance of keeping everything in the context of my relationship with Christ (Psalm 121). Those conversations and key relationships, from middle school through my high school years, impressed on me the importance and necessity of mentorship and Christian discipleship.*

Those mentors included a man who early on invested in Isaiah, allowing him to attend a boarding school and later college, and a counselor at the school who became both friend and advisor, preparing him for his calling to be a youth minister.

In keeping with both how he was shaped and what he believes about forming youth, the ministry he heads now has over 70 teens with upwards of 20 adults, both single and married, who engage each week with them and in special times when school breaks allow time away from their heavy schedules. He describes a typical school year agenda as focusing for the first semester on building deeper relationships with God and with the adults who are part of the ministry, and the second on the questions of living life in this secular culture as a follower of Christ. By this time, the teens have at least one older mentor with whom to work out some of the more difficult questions of life and faith together. All this is based on a very sound theology. He says while fun is always part of what they do, it is not the objective. As he says of his approach;

> *As I continue to walk alongside our middle and high school youth, and as I continue my journey into vocational ministry, I find myself reflecting over the thread of importance that mentorship and discipleship had in me finding myself in Christ. It is one thing to be introduced to Christ and it is a vastly different thing to be guided as you understand what it means to walk with Christ; a walk that is often full of pot holes, swerves and challenging terrain.*

I have come to respect this young man as one of the most winsome and mature young leaders I know, forged in a difficult beginning by mentors God brought into his life to prepare him to turn around and employ the same principles. He may not be an elder quite yet, but he already well understands the role and is recruiting others for this role.

It is in such a church setting that an older person can learn to thrive as a mentor alongside teens or emerging adults. For those who work with the older emerging adults in a church community, they underscore their desire for fostering intergenerational relationships also. In an interview with Derek Melleby of the Center for Parent and Youth Understanding College Initiative, Wheaton College professor David Setran said;

> *... many recognize their need for mentors, guides who can help them make sense of life and call out gifts and passions for vocational use. While it is common for older adults to see those in this age group as a challenge (read trial) to the church, I think it is critical that we also see them as a challenge (read inspiration, motivation, and stimulus) to contemporary church life.*[87]

CALLING ALL (GRAND) PARENTS

Underscoring this thinking of the critical role for elders, University of Southern California professor Vern Bengston has been conducting a longitudinal look at families and faith formation since the 1970s. The conclusions he has arrived at are extremely helpful to

69

our understanding of what ideally should be done if faith is to stick with the next generation and what role we elders might play.[88] His findings are much in agreement with the NSYR studies in affirming the central place of parents in spiritual formation—for good and for ill. Parents are indeed the single greatest spiritual influence on their children. In fact, adolescents today are no less likely to emulate their parents' beliefs than they were in 1970 or 970 BC. Whether it is the choice of religion, intensity of faith, belief in the veracity of the Bible, regularity of participation, idol worship in all its forms, or civic and political engagement, most teens share their parents' perspectives, and this is no different than in all the previous generations. Contrary to some public conclusions concerning the rise of the Nones, the young are not generally abandoning the faith of their parents. What is different today, and *this is a critical distinction*, parents who are essentially Nones in all but name only are more likely passing on their worldview to their children who live it out publicly. Because of the reinforcement from the changes seen in the culture over the last fifty years, this secular hyper-individualism is more comfortable to embrace than the religion that mom and dad are just lukewarm about, Bengston says.

Thus, quite unexpectedly and unique to our modern times, many religious Nones (the 35+% of Americans between the ages of 18-40 who say they have no religious affiliation) have been formed by the previous generation and now are being successful in passing on the faith which they inherited. These younger people did not rebel against their parents for the most part, instead they are mostly following their parents' influence in a tepid or thin faith with no formal church affiliation or one that is very sporadic. Thus, a child's *lack* of religion is often an example of learned religious formation from parents even if they are not aware of it occurring as such.

Often, parents simply want their child to have the *freedom to choose*, which is akin to a sacred cultural belief. Non-theistic or thin-faith families pass down moral and ethical standards just as consistently as pious Jewish, Catholic, or evangelical parents try to pass down their own values and religious standards, and so the trend continues.[89]

What Bengston sees as most influential as to whether older teens remain engaged in their Christian faith are two things:

1. the *intensity* of the beliefs of the parents and
2. the *depth* of the relationship that parents have with their children.

Where parents' faith is uninspired, young people generally do not find it of value to themselves. Where parents' beliefs are strongly expressed and consistently lived out, the influence is far more likely to be transmitted and embraced by their children.

Alongside strong faith lived out daily, the depth of the personal relationship with parents, most particularly with fathers, makes a significant difference, Bengston found. Interestingly, he also found that the faith of *grandparents* is almost as crucial as that of parents, a conclusion my wife and I have come to share as our own formation owes much to the lives and prayers of two Godly grandmothers. This elder generation is a resource seldom discussed in the other literature I've reviewed for my own work, but it underscores the need for elders to remain engaged with youth and young adults, first as grandparents, and then perhaps in *"grandparenting"* others.

The final conclusion Bengston reached would surprise only those unfamiliar with Luke 15.

GOD'S GRANDCHILDREN?

We've all heard the old saw, "God does not have grandchildren." Some young people, as we all have seen, rebel despite the best training by parents and despite the best church or family relationships. They take a different path than they are inculcated in and can become lost or wander away. They waste their spiritual and cultural heritage and often their financial security in the bargain. Parents who continue to love their children through such prodigal times, remaining patient with the door of return open, often find the rebellion is not permanent.

For parents, grandparents, and adult friends of such prodigals,

Bengston says they need to recognize that religion and love are not the same thing. A lot of parents he found personalize the rejection of religion by their children. It is easy to do because anyone who is a parent carries some guilt around about how they wasted time and opportunity before their children are grown. But Bengston admonishes us not to confuse religious conformity with love, and don't confuse a lack of religious conformity with a lack of love.[90] God's Spirit is the power for obedience or change, not religion. That's humbling. Waiting on the Lord so often plays a role in forming the young—despite our desire for quicker change. Churches need the same approach and can be great resources in such cases by linking elders with younger parents to help share the load as mentors and provide wisdom and patience. Many elders have gone through similar tests of time and faith and can offer needed help to younger parents.

In churches, older Christians are needed. Someone like Paul can be a great example.

THE GALATIAN WAY AND MTD

Whether the term is Moralistic Therapeutic Deism (MTD) or juvenilization in culture and in churches, these trends portray something not that unlike the situation Paul encountered on his mission into Galatia. What he had begun with these *baby* Christians was already unraveling as they reached their spiritual teens and emerging adulthood. This prompted his strong response:

> *I am astonished that you are so quickly deserting him who called you in the grace of Christ and are turning to a different gospel—not that there is another one, but there are some who trouble you and want to distort the gospel of Christ. But even if we or an angel from heaven should preach to you a gospel contrary to the one we preached to you, let him be accursed. As we have said before, so now I say again: If anyone is preaching to you a gospel contrary to the one you received, let him be accursed.*[91]

Whatever else MTD is, it is not the gospel and has no power to transform. Thus, what Paul would say candidly to our day is not quite this milder translation "let them be accursed," rather the actual word is *anathema*, better rendered as, "God damn those who teach a watered-down gospel, whether it be of works or of the God who makes me happy." Strong language for a powerful problem, but candor is needed when truth is dumbed down to a watery gruel that has no life in it. Elders need to be able to teach the gospel without distortion and, as J. I. Packer mentored us earlier, elders need to be equipped with such spiritual maturity—also a task (and assignment) for the church to consider in encouraging elders to keep growing spiritually.

The error of the teachers in Galatia which so horrified Paul was the threat of describing believing salvation as centered on oneself and on what one *does* rather than on Christ and what he did by his grace for us at the cross. This was not a mere wordsmithing debate, it was a matter of life or death, and our contemporary *me* theology is also. It is not simply a quirky anomaly of postmodernity but a product of our era's hyper individualism idolatry.

In one form or another, gospel distortion is always the challenge which each age is given to reinterpret in one way or another for their times. The formation of the next generation depends upon protecting the heart of God's love and grace in Christ. Making God all about me and my choices is but the latest religious impulse that results in either false security, indifferent faith, or an eventual drifting away entirely. In the vernacular of the Fuller Youth Institute, a faith anchored in something other than the Truth simply cannot be *sticky*. As elders, we are aiming at what lasts, what sticks for life and that is built on the twin foundations of solid truth and strong relationships of the heart.

COMMUNITIES THAT "WALK BY THE WAY"

We know that for at least half of young Christians, by the time they arrive in the big city for their first jobs, they have been either disillusioned, feel lost and lonely, or have already abandoned the faith of their youth. As they pass by us at the gate we have much work to do, and it is ours to do it as elders in our churches and our communities. To see this responsibility in our age where expressive individualism reigns, recovery of the biblical idea of *koinonia*, community, needs recovery as well. The peer pressure and sheer loneliness often wreak havoc when a young person finds themselves alone in a spiritually strange land. Most often that first move after college is into the major cities to which young Millennials flock. There, finding a new community is critical and elders that care can be part of that new home.

It is in this embodiment of the importance of community in spiritual persistence that Kenda Creasy Dean's insight is helpful for our inquiry about the church. Her conclusion I found to be highly paradoxical coming from an expert in the theology and practice of youth ministry in the church, viz., "*Youth ministry is not accomplished by youth ministers.*" To extrapolate a bit for emerging adults, those between 18 and 30, we can also say that ministry to young Millennials is not necessarily accomplished by ministers of any type—at least not absent a large supporting crew that includes older Christians much like what Isaiah Brooms practices.

Her thinking emerged from years of research and practice and it is cogently described as this:

> "*They [youth or other ministers] seem less effective as catalysts for consequential faith, which is far more likely to take root in the rich relational soil of families, congregations, and mentor relationships where young people can see what faithful lives look like, and encounter the people who love them enacting a larger story of divine care and hope.*"[92]

Translation: simply *attending* church or a demographically focused ministry or parachurch group is not the best answer to the question of forming maturity if deeper spiritual engagement with a wider circle of peers and older mentors is absent.

As a layman, I claim no expertise on the American church as a whole. But here I want to draw from my own church as a place where we are seeking to do this well. Under David Hanke's leadership of Restoration Anglican Church, he stressed from its founding in 2009, that becoming part of a small group is an organic component of being a church member. He teaches that intergenerational relationships are key to a meaningful and growing life. It is within such small communities that mentoring occurs naturally beyond the weekly small group. So, rather than having a *Sunday School* model of instruction for adults, and several *programs* for overscheduled people, the small groups meeting in homes and restaurants and coffee shops during the week serve a catalytic role, particularly for integrating older people with younger. Monthly gatherings of men and women also emphasize how intergenerational mentoring is a priority and they seek to help make that happen.

In metropolitan Washington D.C., like many cities, there are neighborhoods of families bounded by high-rise cliff dwellings of condos and apartments where there is a plurality of single Millennials. Here the intergenerational soil needs such cultivation. As this church plant has grown rapidly, this relational community building strategy of small groups has been central and the encouragement of mentoring remains essential as an organic part of who we are in making disciples. For us it's a work in progress.

The men's small group I am in is the kind of culture that Restoration has sought to create. It is comprised of anywhere from 10-15 guys from every age and marital demographic—20s to 70s—where mentoring takes place within the group on almost every occasion we are together. Someone is usually further down the road of experience when an issue comes up. So by no means is mentoring always one-on-one.

However, it is also the seedbed for such pairings when a business issue arises, a marital difficulty surfaces, a common pornography struggle is discovered, or someone wants to think through retirement—these are all things we have parsed and prayed about together so far with healthy doses of individual mentoring occurring on the side.

For some, perhaps the old saw, "It takes a village to raise a child," comes to mind. That's not quite what I'm trying to get at here. Rather, to borrow a phrase from the Marines, it takes a few good older men and a few good older women, preferably beginning anywhere from their late 30s to their 80s and up, to help build the next generation by becoming mentors. Realistically, those who might qualify as elders in the third third are likely in the best position, as they have time and greater flexibility, if the church will use this resource and not see them as recipients of ministry as J. I. Packer taught us earlier.

Is this starting to resonate? I hope so, but I also hope it does not seem daunting. We are not talking about mentoring as a new five day a week job, but a natural way of life and an organic part of any church—not a program. I want to stress that this reaching back to the next generation is relatively simple, it is intended to be a natural part of life, and is best carried out within a community—it is not just another item on the to-do list or another responsibility on an already overcrowded schedule.

A WORD OF ASSURANCE

Where we are going from here is this: we are going to read some actual stories that demonstrate you do not need to start a new organization or go back to school for another degree to become a mentor. If you are a pastor or leader in a church this is not something that requires a whole new curriculum or dedicated staff, not even a program. The church you are already a part of and the communities you already belong to are where the action is—the most natural place for relationships. The tools are already at hand in your life. The unsung Christian community writ large is the tool container of choice. This also is not a move to replace the role of parents or grandparents, who are our first mentors and examples, or of pastors or ministry leaders who already have a leadership role among us. As an elder, all would welcome your help. Mentors are meant biblically to fulfill the role which surrounds and undergirds and succeeds parents, grandparents, and leaders.

Thus, Kenda Dean rightly observes that "Sociologists [and good theologians] consider *a young person's sense of belonging in a religious community to be a more accurate predictor of his or her adult religious involvement than regular church attendance* (emphasis added)."[93] In other words, putting young Millennial and Gen Z teens, singles, and young marrieds in church pews (or even earlier on youth group beanbags) is one thing, but engagement of the heart and mind, as we have seen in much research on teen and emerging adult faith, is quite another, at least in forming maturing Christians and responsible adults. Feeling a true part of an intergenerational community in some important way, beginning in youth then onward, confers a concomitant sense of budding adulthood upon younger persons. If their community is only other teens or singles or young marrieds, then when they go to college or move to a new city for work, a church will not feel like a new *home*. It is a critical step for a young person to no longer feel they are a child but are becoming an adult member of a wider *koinonia* where having older people to come alongside in daily life is part of the deal.

The good news is the biblical template briefly revisited here is one that we already know still works (as if research was needed to confirm old truths). Just one insight before we get to the stories about mentors: for those 8% who leave high school strong in their faith, "Compared to their peers, [these] young church-attenders are *far more likely to have adults in their lives with whom they enjoy talking, and who give them lots of encouragement* (emphasis added)."[94] They also are very unlikely to become Nones. You will see this played out in the next chapter as the same principle of wisdom holds true for the entire age spectrum of emerging adults.

As we turn now to better understanding the mentoring role we rehearse for all of our lives, be encouraged that this is no less than a calling to those of us who are becoming older or who are already elders. That vocational role is one every elder at the gate has been born to play at some point in life and it does not have to wait until the retirement years. Whether you think of yourself as being mentor material or not, I want to assure you that you are a called, prepared, and ready vessel of God's power to serve just this way. These next stories will show you that is true.

Chapter 7

Stories From Those Who Pass by the Gate

I have been fortunate to have a number of mentors over the years; some spiritual, some not-so-much, but the common thread in all of these relationships was that they took an interest in me and were committed to my progress.
Doug, retired Air Force fighter pilot, grandfather, and rocket engineer

One of the things I have learned in my life is that if I want to really understand someone, I need to talk with their friends, their colleagues, their subordinates, their family, because most of us don't have a complete perspective on ourselves. While there are a few, very few, basic guidelines for mentoring which we will get to later, I place much more value on real stories. So, I asked a number of people to give me their mentor stories—what did their mentors do and what were they like as people that made such an impression on your life?

I was a bit surprised that people really wanted to tell these stories almost as a way to say thank you to those that helped to shape them. Like Doug, most spoke of something selfless in their mentors, sort of a combination of putting them before themselves and passing on something that would help them grow more mature, more wise.

If you are considering taking up this call to mentor, listen carefully because you can hear something of a vision for what you might be about as you grow into your elder role. There are three common threads or themes that knit their varied experiences together.

79

The Gift of Time

Not surprisingly, some told about their parents or grandparents. Steve, a university professor and writer, spoke of his father:

"When I was an adolescent, about 14 years old, one evening we talked about why he wasn't going to the laboratory that night. Without a hint of criticism of others, he simply said that his understanding of life called him to more than *getting ahead* by doing more research and writing. He wanted to be on the school board, an elder in his church, at work in the local prison, and a father to his sons—so he wouldn't be back in the lab that night, or most other nights. That was my father's gift to me, looking over his shoulder and through his heart as I did."

Steve's dad made a conscious choice to use the scarcest resource in his possession, time, and gave it to his son. As a father himself and a grandfather of 10 now, he can see what that sacrifice meant—an example he follows now as a mentor to countless college students and emerging adults. Steve also wrote a seminal book[95] about mentors who help sustain faith in the young that has been central in my own understanding.

Brooks, a chemist, father of three youngsters, wrote this about his grandmother:

"One of the most important characteristics of my grandmother was that she was available to spend time with me. Conversations here and there with admirable people are great, but they are thin compared to years of close connection with someone who would sit down with you whenever you happened to show up. After I moved away, we spoke less frequently. I was no longer a few houses away and was no longer available. She always was. She died about a month before the birth of my first son, Ian. I was able to tell her Ian's name before she passed. She repeated it over and over through her oxygen mask."

Brooks is an amazing dad and husband today, so for those who are grandparents or aspire to be one someday, never underestimate your place in the lives of your grandchildren. While I can attest to the joy that role has for us, pouring yourself in simple ways into their lives cannot be overestimated in its formational value even to the next generation.

Still, it is one thing for family to be generous with time, but in an overly busy world, we sometimes think it's an imposition on others. Danny, newly married, a young dad, and government statistician wrote about Andrew, a man who had prayed for this fatherless young boy for over a year before they ever met more formally. Here is what struck him as he looked back:

"Andrew's magic trick that I will never understand was how he fit 30 hours of responsibilities and pursuits into a 24-hour day. He met regularly with at least five men throughout the month, served as a church elder, was a CFO, without sacrificing time with his wife and three kids. So the couple of hours he gave me every other Tuesday were invaluable. Over the course of almost two years, he canceled our time together less than five times, and those few cancellations were rescheduled. At least once a quarter, he had me at his home eating his wife's cooking."

Kate is a newly married family nurse practitioner and committed to a mission to a community in South America in her spare time. We were privileged to spend time with her and her husband before they were married and since. I knew she must have someone in her life that helped make her into the amazing young woman we know. I was not disappointed. It all began in high school as she tells it.

"I was initially drawn towards my mentor, Christine, because of the zest and passion she inspired in the classroom. She was my creative writing teacher in high school. She desired to know what inspired her students and what they aspired to be. We remained in touch when I went off to college and I entered my profession. I will always be grateful that she sought me out and invited me into her life. She made time for me when I came home for holidays and we spent hours over coffee and pastries discussing everything from faith to relationships to books to careers. She felt like a kindred

81

spirit and was living the way that I could envision myself living 25 years later, which is why I actively seek out her advice and input now. I admired the way she poured into her students, cherished her family, served her community, traveled the globe, and read voraciously. I also admired the way she was still constantly seeking personal and spiritual growth of her own and never acted like she had already figured everything out. It was incredibly valuable to hear from a female adult who was not my own mother. It was like a window into a world that I wouldn't otherwise be invited into. Our mentorship dynamic was never formal. There was no clear start or end. She may even be surprised to know that I call her my mentor. I was simply drawn to her warmth and encouragement and the way she emitted love and light in the world. I will be forever grateful for her guidance and our friendship."

All service requires sacrifice, so it's probably best to be honest and say that when you mentor someone, it takes time to build a deep heart relationship, time away from other things you might do, but also recognize from what these stories represent that the gift of your time (and your heart) is perhaps the best way you can say to someone, "You are important to me, I love you and want to give you this gift." There may be no better investment.

The Gifts of Honesty and Transparency

As I look back over the pages and pages of mentor stories, what people seemed to esteem most highly was honesty, even when it was a bit painful or awkward. I think why this is so is that honesty is accepted more easily from someone who is not related—and I qualify this—as long as there is transparency alongside. Here is where heart work occurs and iron sharpens iron. Al, a retired Air Force major general, wrote about Dick, an older pilot he worked with, whose advice about all aspects of life was a natural outflow of their working relationship. "Dick was an open and honest storyteller, and he shared his personal successes and some not so successful stories. His interest in me and his advice were personally very motivating to me. I admired his candor, success, hard work, and commitment. We stayed in touch for years." Today, Al says that as an elder at the gate he emulates what Dick did with him.

Adam, a political consultant and father of three, told about his college mentor who shared his stories: "Victories, failures, passions, apathies—I heard them all. He challenged me to change some things but focused more on encouraging me in the positive. We would talk through accountability issues together. It was never one-sided. I always appreciated that."

Adam highlights one particularly important practice—the impact of mutual honesty and transparency which set the stage for his accountability relationship. Often, accountability is something you will find people are actually looking for in a mentor, particularly in overcoming habits or besetting sinful behavior. Obviously, this is a place of great personal trust, a product of humility when sharing all of your life provides not only wisdom but engenders a deep confidence. When we trust others with our own soft spots, they realize that we can be trusted with their failures and challenges as well.

David, a pastor and father of four, has a story to share that shows how mutual honesty and transparency opened up greater opportunity for life change. After college he was involved in campus ministry and met Brian, who was his supervisor, mentor, and friend, who figures in this story:

"Brian and I both play guitar. When our team created regional conferences for students, we were pretty deficient in musical worship leaders, so Brian and I would often lead together. At one point, Brian turned to me and to the rest of the staff team and said, 'David is a better guitar player and worship leader than I. I am asking him to take on musical worship leadership at our camps and conferences. I will serve on the music team but under his leadership.' It was a powerful moment of promotion in the best sense of the word. He used his authority for the good of the students in the region and to create an opportunity for me to grow in my gifts."

Brian's humility and honesty with the leadership team about his own abilities was a powerful lesson for David's life that allowed him to entrust his own heart to Brian later in a very difficult turning point in his life. Here is how he tells it:

"Brian taught me about what it means to lead and supervise people. He set an incredibly high bar for what it looks like to *know* your employees or mentees. In the early years of my marriage, I was stuck in a habit of pornography. In the fall of 2009, things were very broken in my relationship with myself, with Laurel, and with God. Laurel and I were considering a separation. We had a relationship of trust with Brian and I confessed to him what was happening. Brian was very concerned about me, about my students, and about my marriage. He was able to articulate the idolatry that was at work in my life—that I was seeking something that would make me feel ok about myself. My first idol was Laurel; and if she did not affirm me enough my second idol was ministry to students; and if they did not affirm me enough my third idol was pornography—and it always provided a fantasy that I was wanted, and the shame to deaden any of my other insecurities. Those three idols were insatiable and they were destroying my soul. Brian's discernment was this: he did not want me to lose my marriage and he wanted it to get healthier and not be idolatrous. It was unclear that I was willing to give up my idol of pornography, but if I worked hard there were tools to help. The only idol that Brian could control was my idolatry of my role as a pastor to students, so as an act of grace and mercy, Brian gave (and required) me to take an 8-month paid leave of absence from Intervarsity. He took away my access to the idol of ministry so that I could work on my idolatry of Laurel and pornography. That decision came at financial and strategic cost to Brian, and it was unclear at the beginning if it would make any measurable difference. But at the end of the eight months (and now looking back 15 years later) it was the *gift* that saved my marriage, my future in vocational ministry, and maybe my relationship with Jesus. Brian was brave, sacrificial, and loving."

And, I would add, honest—he spoke the truth in love that only by a radical change which would cost both men could this tough decision have any chance of success. Today, David, whom you've already met, is one of the single finest men I know, an amazing leader, my pastor, and as I remind him, I will entrust him to care for my family and bury me one day. Without Brian, there might be no David in my life.

THE GIFT OF SERVING

For several years I taught and consulted to several organizations on the development of their leaders. When I first began, I wanted to better answer two questions for myself so I could teach others:

1. Why do people follow leaders willingly?
2. How do you grow such leaders?

To get at these answers, I often began a seminar with a simple exercise. I would ask for two volunteers and place them in front with two flip charts to record the audience responses. The scenario I gave them was this: two former leaders they had worked for each has a new initiative they are heading and they call you to see if you're interested in joining them. The first one you would move heaven and earth for and leave as soon as possible to help them to get the job done. The second one you would run kicking and screaming away from: never again would you work for them. Alternating between the two charts, I'd ask the audience for one or two words that best describe both leaders. It was what I'd call the Great Leader/Lousy Leader Exercise. After having done this at least half a hundred times, I could predict the outcome. Great leaders cared, they were humble, they put others before themselves. Lousy leaders were those who were arrogant, selfish, and narcissistic. Character more than competence shone above all. Elsewhere, I have also written from my experience and research that leaders grow leaders as exemplars, coaches, teachers, and, of course, mentors.[96] So it is no surprise that servant leadership or at least a willingness to serve others was a prominent part of the stories I heard. That may be the most prominent part of Jesus' character that is valued in a mentor. Even Thomas Jefferson saw this.

Most people if they hear the story of the life of Jesus find him to be exemplary. Thomas Jefferson, though a Unitarian who constructed his own "bible" free of miracles, still had this to say this about Jesus:

> *In extracting the pure principles which he taught, we should have to strip off the artificial vestments in which they have been muffled by priests, who have travestied them into various forms, as instruments of riches and power to them... There will be found remaining the most benevolent code of morals which has ever been offered to man. I have performed this operation for my own use by cutting verse by verse out of the printed book, and arranging the matter which is evidently his, and which is easily distinguishable as diamonds in a dunghill.[97]*

Jefferson, who loved to describe himself as just a humble servant of the people, certainly drew upon one of Jesus' most memorable teachings to his disciples (and us) on how to behave as leaders (or mentors for that matter) which is often described as *servant-leadership*. Jesus offered this teaching to those who would lead the church after him shortly before his death. The occasion was a dispute among them as to who was the greatest of the inner circle of twelve.

> *You know that those who are considered rulers of the Gentiles lord it over them, and their great ones exercise authority over them. But it shall not be so among you. But whoever would be great among you must be your servant, and whoever would be first among you must be slave of all. For even the Son of Man came not to be served but to serve, and to give his life as a ransom for many.[98]*

It was not just Jesus' teaching that served to shape the followers he spent three years in daily mentoring. It was his example of service, giving his very life, which remained with them, that and the gift of time spent during those rich years.

Louisa, now a teacher and mother of three, spoke of the example of her mentor, Melanie, who entered her life shortly after she was married. As she tells the story, she and her husband moved to Mississippi four days after their wedding and with all the changes in her life and being raised in a somewhat dysfunctional family, she had lots of uncertainties about how to be a wife. So when she met Melanie in the small church they attended, Louisa reached out and asked her to be her mentor. This was a woman who was seemingly perfect, always put together, possessing Godly character with a love for theology. As the mother of three grown girls, she "had a plan" as Louisa said, for a happy home and carried it out each day. They met regularly on Tuesdays for a couple of hours where they read books or listened to tapes together, almost all of it about marriage and following God in all things. Melanie became "like a mom," Louisa said, providing her favorite snacks seasoned with encouragement and love. She even adopted Melanie's six priorities for life that they learned from an important book they studied together. Those standards remained in place for many years afterward until life became more complex. Today, Louisa is among the few older women in a very young congregation and is mentor to other young moms just as she was once helped. As a high school teacher, she also spends personal time with the younger girls, helping to form who they are as well as to develop a love for reading good literature.

David, a senior executive and father of four, spoke of Michael, his boss, as a model of what he wants to be for others.

"Michael, as a Mexican American, was the only ethnic minority division leader in an organization that could best be described as a cut-throat, competitive culture where failure wasn't tolerated. This backdrop is important in understanding the mentor-mentee relationship I developed with Michael. *Michael taught me how to create a (healthy) sub-culture within a corporate culture.* His primary responsibility was to protect his unit from a culture that treated its employees as merely full-time equivalents (FTEs), where lowering your labor-to-revenue ratio was a key objective. Michael set out to create a culture in the transportation unit that valued individuals and had the mission to solve intractable government problems like traffic congestion. His 1,000+ employees found fulfillment and fun in spite of the overall corporate culture. *Michael was the most compassionate man I have ever met in corporate life.* I can't remember a year working for Michael where there weren't layoffs, and our group was never spared in spite of its growth. Michael made sure that each individual was treated with respect, and I even remember one instance when he (and I) came to tears over a layoff discussion. As a result, I never heard an unkind word about Michael from an employee or a customer. *There was no clear separation of faith and family from work with Michael.* We all knew Michael's wife and son, where he went to church, the Boy Scout troop he led, and the vacations he took. The management team would often go over to each other's houses and our families all got along. I compare that to other executives, where the extent of my knowledge of their personal life was the family photo on their desk. *Michael exhibited a "Level 5 Leader" blend of extreme personal humility with intense professional will.* Michael never boasted about his remarkable track record, in fact he never exhibited arrogance. I think most would say that one of his greatest attributes was his humility. I would like to say he passed that down to me, but I don't think others would agree. *I learned how to be a mentor and a coach from Michael.* He taught me that you shouldn't be a manager if you aren't willing to coach (and mentor). We expect nothing less from coaches in professional sports, why should we allow executives to focus on self-preservation and who think of management as an Excel spreadsheet. Michael and I remain close friends even after he left. I only hope that I can live up to his example of an exceptional mentor and leader."

We tend to think that imparted wisdom is what mentoring is all about, and perhaps worry whether we have the goods. Certainly, in small ways and large, advice about living a good life was in every story of every person I interviewed. But over and over it seems the lasting impression is one of the willingness of mentors to pour their lives into others as examples of how to follow Christ in the crucible of real life that shaped who they became. This quality of selfless service and caring, in one way or the other, came up most often.

Bill, a young father of three and a high school teacher spoke with great appreciation for the way his mentor, Jeff, poured his life into him in almost weekly one-on-ones.

"We talked about all of life, but almost always through the lens of our relationship with Jesus. Jeff often started our times by asking what I had been reading during my quiet times or what was on my mind. Through these questions and through hearing his own reflections, I learned what it meant to walk with God, listen for His voice in Scripture, and see my life as an opportunity to share the joy and love of God with others. Many of our discussions centered around sharing my faith, living in community with Christians and non-Christians alike, understanding my heart and beliefs about myself and in turn what Jesus had to say about me. We rarely talked theology in the sense of addressing tough questions about Christianity. Instead, the meetings were almost always pastoral. We always prayed together, and I knew deeply that his desire for me was to walk closely with Jesus. His willingness and commitment to meeting with me was striking."

One litmus test, I believe, for each of these relationships is whether the younger person takes up the role of mentor themselves as they journey toward being an elder. They forge strong links with those that went before and then are prepared to serve those coming behind. Not surprisingly, this was a consistent reflection. For Bill, this is what it looks like in his life now:

"Over the past two summers, I have worked with 4-5 college students during a summer work program. Part of my responsibility has been to meet with them weekly, and I often find myself channeling Jeff during these times. I love meeting with these young men and have found it to be a great grace for me, as well as an encouragement for them. In thinking about all that Jeff did for me, I think the traits that stand out strongest are his own love of Jesus, his humility, his boldness, and his commitment to me."

For Doug, a fellow elder at the gate, Bob was the older man he aspired to become, and the time spent and his example over a long period continues to shape him today.

"Bob took an immediate interest in my spiritual development and offered to meet monthly for lunch and conversation. He challenged me to memorize Scripture and go deeper in my faith, asking me if I had ever tried writing out my testimony or sharing my faith publicly (I hadn't!). Over the next fifteen years, Bob and I met regularly and saw each other at church. His quiet example as a father, husband, and churchman made a big impression me and helped me tremendously in my spiritual growth. Again, this was a blessing that God seemed to drop in my lap. I didn't seek the relationship with Bob; it found me."

THE MAKING OF A MENTOR

One of the outcomes of being a mentor may be unseen in this life, a seed sown that grows and you may never experience in full bloom. That is how the generation to generation links work.

For Heather, an Air Force officer and mother of two, her mentor was a high-level executive who had major responsibilities in an international health organization and in raising a family. Her example of managing often conflicting responsibilities has taught Heather to emulate her as she has gained rank, higher level experience, and grew a family. She has now turned around and become a mentor, herself.

"I really focus on taking time for people, usually younger officers and work to be available for questions or a listening ear. I've also made it a priority for those under me to professionally mentor them. This desire has also encouraged me to start a women officers luncheon group, to give other women a forum to start friendships or mentorships and build a group of possible advice-givers in an environment where there are less than 20% women."

Alan was someone I particularly wanted to consult with on this question of who his mentors were, as his life's work has been as a mentor to dozens of young men in South Africa, intentionally seeking to prepare them for post-apartheid leadership since the 1990s. Everywhere he goes he seeks out young men to meet with and to pour his life into. I would describe him as a mentor's mentor. His story of who mentored him I knew would be particularly rich so I've saved it as the penultimate one. I share it here in almost its entirety:

"The first one is Isaac Balie, my high school teacher and the one who helped me to understand the importance of having a personal relationship with Jesus. After my confession of faith he bought me a Bible and showed me how to read it and do Bible study. He modeled to me that being a Christian is being different—everything changes. He was uncompromising in his faith.

My second mentor was Bill Kiser, a guy I met at university. He took an interest in me and... showed that our faith is not for ourselves—not to sit in a holy huddle. He showed me how to have fun and still be committed as a Christian. The greatest gift he imparted was modeling how I can have a personal ministry: how to share the gospel with others one on one, how to lead a small group, etc.

Nduba Mazabani mentored me and showed me that I have ability to lead others, including white people. Growing up in apartheid South Africa, it was drilled into you that you must stay with your own and lead your own. Ndaba believed differently, he believed in his ability as a person. He made me believe in myself that I can lead people of all races.

My fourth mentor was a woman. Her name is Joan Campbell. She took me into her home as a boarder. She was in her sixties when I met her—well educated and with a brilliant mind, but she walked humbly and had a strong inner life. She listened to the soul. She prayed, she listened more than gave answers; she never judged. A woman of prayer, she understood that the inner life is what anchors you, not all that you say and do. Oh, and she taught me some manners and social etiquette which stood me in good stead when I started to court my wife."

With four mentors like that, it is no wonder Alan remains focused on forging links with the next generations and likely will until he is home.

A FINAL ENCOURAGEMENT

In closing, not everyone I interviewed had stories to tell about those who mentored them. Still, I wanted to include this one last story as Greg, now an airline pilot and one of the finest dads I know, had some wisdom to share that I think might encourage you as you consider your role at or nearing the gate. Oh, and he does note one mentor every married man ought to credit.

"When I think back on whom specifically I would write about—I come up blank. Not that I didn't have opportunities to develop mentors, but I never really cultivated a formal mentoring relationship. I wasn't counseled at the time on the wisdom of doing so. In fact, I was raised in an environment that elevated self-sufficiency and a healthy skepticism of others' motives over information sharing and reliance on other people. Yet I'm still blessed. While I regret not building more formal mentors, I succeeded in cultivating a few great friends in whom I could hold great confidence and trust unconditionally. Indeed, I keep my best mentor as close as possible—I married her. I have spent the last twenty years bouncing ideas and decisions off of her; it's her counsel that kept me on track to continue my Air Force career; she introduced me to a formal spiritual life—now I'm active on our church's Council; she steered us to the DC area—a decision that has brought us profound happiness as we are raising our family amongst wonderful friends, neighbors, and family. I think the great benefit of your project won't be to show younger adults why they should seek mentors—that ought to be obvious—but as they age, it will teach them to how to build mentoring partnerships and seek outlets for their wisdom."

I think Greg's point is a good one to underscore. For those who are coming up, mentoring often (not always) works best when it is your initiative, when you sense an older person can speak into your life and you recognize it is needed. The risk is worth it. For those who are in a position to reach back to the next generation, be aware that sometimes younger people hang back for a variety of reasons like Greg's, and a simple invitation may be all that is needed. These stories are meant as an encouragement that each of us can become part of the stories of others, stories that have been written from the foundation of the world.[99] It is well to reiterate, what younger people are looking for is the wisdom of elders. Wisdom is far less advice however as we have seen it is more of the heart, a whole life shared with time given and taken to know each other well so that the love of Christ may come to the fore. Being a mentor is not playing Dear Abby. It is more like Paul and Timothy, or Naomi and Ruth.

Mentors have their own stories as well, insights gained from their time sitting by the gate. For my money, these next stories are truly heart wisdom.

CHAPTER 8

STORIES FROM THOSE WHO SIT AT THE GATE

*If a man has a stubborn and rebellious son who will not obey
the voice of his father or the voice of his mother, and, though they
discipline him, will not listen to them, then his father and his
mother shall take hold of him and bring him out to the elders of
his city at the gate of the place where he lives, and they shall say
to the elders of his city, 'This our son is stubborn and rebellious; he
will not obey our voice; he is a glutton and a drunkard.'*[100]

Elders at the gate did more than act as legal counsel or settle
contracts, they were there for times when unresolvable issues hit
families. In the formative days of the new nation of Israel, the
connection between rebellion in the youth and a potential national
crisis was recognized as a given. We already learned that lesson
from Wisdom in Proverbs.

Like most in my generation, the first national crisis which I
remember vividly was the assassination of President John F. Kennedy in 1963. I was a 20-year old senior at the Air Force Academy
and can well recall the sense of thunderstruck shock as two thousand young men suddenly went silent as the news was announced
during lunch. Within a few hours I was being mobilized to march
as part of the honor guard that accompanied his body to its resting
place in Arlington National Cemetery. It all seemed so surreal.

But the crisis of my older years, one that shapes our times still,
was so unimaginable that it is a day burned most deeply into my

mind, what we now simply refer to as 9/11. The endless replays of planes flying into two buildings, the smoke and then the burning followed by the slow, implosive collapse, all the while watching with horror as bodies came flying from windows like birds scattering in the air though they never rose before disappearing. And then came the apocalyptic, volcanic, roiling dust clouds that engulfed the screen as terror-stricken observers fled the onrush down the empty streets.

These images often pop up at odd times in my thoughts because in the aftermath, what still gives me chills, is the heroic stories of the first responders that began to emerge. They are the stories of the firemen and policemen and then the hard hats, all what we call *ordinary* people that somehow redeemed this event from a senseless act of terrorism to one of deep significance. For a brief time, we saw the best of humanity, we came together as a nation, and across the country, rich and poor, many flooded into churches to pray. A rare moment. There was even a seeming miracle as a ghostly, steel girder cross emerged from the rubble. The dust-covered hard hats asked a priest to bless it perhaps as a talisman of safety, if not a sign of new life.

Peggy Noonan's account in *The Wall Street Journal* describes being among the many upscale, numbed New Yorkers gathered on the streets, applauding with pride the brave men who were daily heading to restore order from the smoldering chaos. For her, this tragedy came to have a deeper, underlying meaning which she asked us to reflect upon:

> *It is not only that God is back, but that men are back. A certain style of manliness is once again being honored and celebrated in our country since September 11. You might say it suddenly emerged from the rubble of the past quarter century, and emerged when a certain kind of man came forth to get our great country out of the fix it was in.*
>
> *I am speaking of masculine men, men who push things and pull*

things and haul things and build things, men who charge up the stairs in a hundred pounds of gear and tell everyone else where to go to be safe. Men who are welders, who do construction, men who are cops and firemen. They are all of them, one way or another, the men who put the fire out, the men who are digging the rubble out, and the men who will build whatever takes its place.

And their style is back in style. We are experiencing a new respect for their old-fashioned masculinity, a new respect for physical courage, for strength, and for the willingness to use both for the good of others.[101]

Of course she did not mean this as a gender rant, rather it is a story about the recovery of *responsibility*, a description of those certain times in life when a crisis occurs and the human response becomes a moral choice—either flight or fight—a character test brought about within the instinctive reflex choice of whether to run to the danger in disregard of oneself... or not.

As I've thought much about what is happening among the younger generations in an age some call a new spiritual dark age,[102] I wonder if this picture of the first responders can help us here to better see something that might be speaking to those who are becoming older or have arrived at that place by the gate. Not only is this a time of chaos, secularity, and deep anxiety, but it is a time when it is the older people particularly that are needed to run toward the difficult, toward the formation of the responsible maturity of character. Elders and all those who are becoming elders are needed to be heroes.

The singular change of the delay of a decade in young people taking their place as responsible adults significantly alters the playing field for would-be mentors more than any generation before us. I don't think that it is an exaggeration given what we've discussed thus far. The choice is to put ourselves in harm's way, so to speak, by being *at the gate* where the next generation is passing to address this crisis of the young, or to retreat into a good retirement where life is easier and we check off the things we want to do before we die.

As you consider your own time in life right now or in a few years and your responsibilities to help meet the needs that are there for the generations that follow, I want to offer further encouragement in some life stories of others to draw upon. Those who are or have been mentors can be our teachers. To begin, this is perhaps my favorite historical mentoring story, the one that got me thinking far more about my own responsibility.

WILBERFORCE AND NEWTON

One of the most remarkable stories of the impact of an older mentor on a younger person was that of the English slave trader turned preacher, John Newton, and his decades-long relationship with a wealthy, young politician, William Wilberforce, who was destined to secure the abolition of slavery in Britain and its colonies. When Wilberforce's father died, he was but nine and to add to this shock, his mother had a breakdown.

Providentially, his care fell to his uncle and aunt in London where the lad became part of their family's circle of friends, "Enthusiasts" they were derisively called, those who had converted to Methodism under the preaching of George Whitfield. Young William soon became an ardent follower alarming his grandfather and mother. But before they could call him home, Newton had taken the boy under his wing, treating him as a son.

Though Wilberforce later regressed during his later teens (sound familiar?) to the gaming, drinking, card playing life of a young gentleman, as he grew older, his precocious entry to Parliament and fame at the age of 21 did not bring him peace. He was finally led to repent of his ways and felt drawn to leave the dirty business of politics in favor of becoming a clergyman. But seeking out his boyhood mentor after many years of avoidance, he badly needed Newton's vocational advice. Confounding Wilberforce's intentions, Newton instructed him to take on the slave trade industry instead of a collar and remain in politics where he was needed far more.

That conversation fixed the course of Wilberforce's life which he would later describe as a dual calling: to reform the crude, selfish English culture and to end the trade entirely. Even so, after ten years of futile battle, Wilberforce became exhausted and thought a better man was needed. Newton, now an old man, would have none of it. In the movie version of this incredible story, Newton sends him off with this admonition: "Go Wilber, go, we have lots of work to do you and I."

Though it took yet another ten years, the bill to abolish the slave trade passed Parliament in July 1807. Four months later, John Newton died. Though blind at the end, he was given the gift of "seeing" what he and his young friend Wilber had achieved in the work they did together for over 20 years: one who prayed, advised, held accountable, and encouraged while the other labored in the crucible of leading the nation's great change from slavery to freedom, from selfishness to compassion. That set the stage for Wilberforce and his followers to take on slavery itself.

Many of those whom he had mentored now came to the fore to labor unceasingly for another 27 years to end the evil practice entirely. That effort was led by the young Quaker, Thomas Buxton, whom Wilberforce mentored then passed on the mantle of leadership to launch the legal challenge. But even when he later retired from Parliament due to poor health, Wilberforce was still active in the cause as an advisor. At the end, even as his life faded, he finally received the joyous confirmation of the success of abolition from a young colleague as he lay on his deathbed. The circle was complete.[103]

The Gathering of a Wise Council

I must admit, what Wilberforce and Newton did together to usher in the Victorian era of societal change is perhaps a daunting illustration for us to begin with. Still, after a 35-year career in public service, I see in them the possibilities for us in our fractious, narcissistic, and paralyzed times as an example of the valuable role of a mentor. The tender letters Newton wrote Wilberforce over the years convey how often he prayed and how deeply they connected at a heart level. As we draw upon a few elders at the gate who are already engaged in one way or the other in mentoring others, you might find not just inspiration here but some way forward for yourself within their stories. These are people with a passion for their latter years calling.

Preferably, I would have sat down with all of them in a beautiful location, a retreat in the mountains perhaps, then invite every one of you to come join the circle for a discussion, one that might last for a few days. There, we could all listen to the good, the bad, and the ugly tales of what they are doing, what drew them to finish their lives by investing in the next generation, what they have learned in the process, and how excited they are when they talk. I know there would be a buzz in the room as they compared notes about what they love to do and with who. But absent that, I've convened this council of seven older men and women on these pages whom I can safely say are distinguished as elders at the gate, following Newton's and Wilberforce's examples. I've talked to most of them, personally, and it was hard for some of us to hang up after talking about all this. There is energy in the room, trust me. But first, let me introduce them to you.

Gary Brown along with his wife, Joani, have long had a desire to see people flourish where they are planted. He was a successful custom builder while they raised six children. In their work and family life, mentoring younger people was something they just did. But then they felt called to form Alumni Connect,[104] a non-profit organization whose purpose is to connect college graduates with older mentors in the new cities they settle into for their first time on the stage of life. Talk to them and you get a sense of what zeal for mentoring is all about and how they love the relationships they have built and the connections they have been able to forge with mentors.

Morna Comeau is currently the Program Development Director for The Fellows Initiative (TFI),[105] a network of 25 (and growing) local Fellows Programs in Christian churches across the country and the longtime Director of the Fellows Program at The Falls Church Anglican. TFI is a post-college initiative in local, church-based places where they facilitate the launching of a select group of recent college graduates into diverse careers and life responsibilities with a year of preparation. They receive the support of seminary level teaching, an internship, a home to live in, and parallel job and life coaching—and a mentor for the year. Several of my students or younger friends have been blessed by this amazing initiative.

Anne Cregger, my dear friend whom I introduced earlier, leads The Navigators Nav20s[106] DC Program which she launched in 2010. She spends most of her time meeting with emerging adults searching for greater connection with God, meaning, and others of like minds as they begin their careers after college. Before then she led a Fellows program for ten years and then was a consultant to government organizations on mentoring programs. It's like her whole life prepared her for the place she is in now. I wish you could see her eyes shine as she talks about the young adults she spends so much time with. She's married and is also the mom of four grown boys and an enthusiastic grandmother.

Bruce Fister is a retired Air Force Lieutenant General and former Special Operations Commander who recently stepped down from leading the Officers Christian Fellowship[107] for ten years. He also is mining his life experiences in leading others by writing a blog and a book, *Growing and Building: Faith, Prayer, and Leadership*.[108] He's been married over 50 years and is the father of two grown boys and a granddad.

Kay Hotaling and her husband, Kent, married for 59 years, were involved for a long time with The Fellowship in Washington and were also engaged in the African reconciliation effort. They have three grown sons, and a large part of her life has often involved mentoring younger women. Today she and her husband meet monthly to encourage Young Life[109] staff at their home in Oregon.

Rick Woolworth is a 35-year veteran of Wall Street and founder of Telemachus[110] where he and his wife Jill connect and mentor high potential men and women, both singles and couples, from ages 25 to 40. Through hosting small conferences, workshops, and other events, emerging leaders forge inter-generational friendships with experienced leaders in the Telemachus community Rick has built, so they can together tackle challenging life issues openly and honestly in strong friendships.

Nancy Ziegler has led Bible studies for women for decades and has also served as a frequent mentor to younger women through the C. S. Lewis Fellows Program.[111] She is the mother of two grown daughters and a grandmother as well as a late in life artist.[112]

With those formalities out of the way, let's sit down and talk. We'll start with the basics.

First of all, I asked, how do these experienced mentors initially connect with those they mentor? As it turns out, they describe it in three different ways—sometimes at the initiative of the younger person, sometimes at the initiative of the elder, but then sometimes through a third party who makes the connection. For those who connect through a program or ministry, the relationship comes through the process of assigning a mentor such as The Fellows Initiative typically does or as the C. S. Lewis Institute Fellows program does in giving some choice of mentor from a few available. But for the more informal relationships, it seems most take the first step themselves and maybe that's a matter of personality. Anne Cregger for example says,

> It's hard to say because it's so organic. I come across them in my normal life and work: through church or the Fellows Programs or through the online access that Navigator grads have to Nav20s in cities. Or it can also be people I know from living here so long (friends of my own kids or children of my friends). Or we just have mutual friends, how most people meet. And finally, there are those whose parents or friends call from a different city to specifically ask me to connect with their young person (friend, niece, son, daughter,

protégé, etc.) because they're having a particular difficulty in the DC area. But whatever the path, it usually starts with me asking them if they'd like to grab coffee sometime. Sometimes it's initiated by them, but more often it's me.

Bruce Fister agrees but says the next meeting is up to the person he has met with as they tend to have much busier lives and he wants them to take the initiative and not just be polite about continuing. It is important that if this relationship is to go deeper to the heart level, it has to be a priority for both.

It's also fair to conclude that everyone agrees that outside of a structured program, no one tries to formally name this as mentoring or to make the agreement official. It's just understood that this is a growing relationship and that prayer and growing in faith are integral to any issue they address.

I also wanted to talk about why young people seek out an older person in the first place. What our council agreed was that this need for an elder in their life is very evident in today's young people, a need that can't be Googled. We've said earlier that heart to heart relationships with wise elders comes as a natural part of who we are as people made by God, but that today's culture has barriers to what is needed. Kay Hotaling says most of the women she has mentored have been younger marrieds who have sought her out as they encounter the challenges of marriage. But she also says that some have even told her later she had really helped them without any awareness on her part this had occurred, simply that they had built a friendship and the results were a byproduct. Her insight is that, "They're looking for the perspective/wisdom they think an older person might have for them, or they're looking for a safe place to deal with personal issues." But note that such safety in being transparent with personal issues is not found in casual encounters or one-off meetings. It takes time to build the heart connections which younger people cherish as a gift.

Morna Comeau, on the other hand, works mostly with younger

single women, and her experience is, "They seem interested in knowing an older adult who is *not* related or a friend of their mother's—someone who will be real with them. They are also very curious about marriage," since relationships for singles are near the top of what they often want to discuss.

As an aside, I throw in that for the younger, single guys I mentor, I'd say it's not much different except they seem to get serious about their marriage interest later than the young women Morna mentors. A common complaint.

But vocational issues for younger people definitely make the short list, too. Bruce and Rick find most of their mentoring centers around things like leadership, career, and life balance. Bruce says that, "The most common reason is that people want to draw upon my leadership experience within a Christian context. Most issues concern handling people and interfacing with their greater organization."

Rick says he probably sees more Type As who are hard-charging but recognize the price paid in family life and the stress takes a toll. I love some wise advice he passed on during an intergenerational Stanford Business School program he attended that typifies his approach in a very secular setting:

> *Seek clarity as to how you determine your True North/Moral Compass/Non-negotiables. Make sure this compass is pointed toward that which is bigger than yourself—hopefully, transcendent. If you don't, you will likely 'come to the end of yourself' at some point in your life. I did, in my late 40s. Think deeply as to what is success. Don't let the culture define it for you. Imagine it is your 80th birthday and family and friends will be honoring you tonight at a dinner. Write out five brief things you hope people will say about you. This is an excellent proxy for what is long-term success. Once completed, over the years ask yourself if the way you are leading your life is on this path.*

He told me in that pretty eclectic Millennial group of B School scholars he got an ovation afterward. Honest truth is compelling. Note that he has opened himself and his heart to them, not as a superior but as someone who wrestled with the meaning of success in life. He also shares how a different perspective—how you want to look back at your life—can change the choices you make today. You can see why this elder who has had worldly success can build a deeper relationship as he is humble and approachable.

For Morna Comeau, the Fellows programs typically meet more with younger people at the beginning of their careers, so the questions are often about making the right initial choices. They have an entire year to build the kind of mentoring relationships that allows for the older people that volunteer in the program to speak into the trajectory that the younger folks take afterward.

Personally, I find that there is too much stress upon young people to decide on the exact right vocation that they were meant and made to do (I surely resembled that). I try to get them to relax and make the best seeming early choice, then *live into* their work over a period of a few years while they learn more about themselves. Change of careers is more the norm than not and it's not a tragedy to do so. I try to help them see, as I did, that God is not testing you to see if you guess correctly. Here, lots of conversation and prayer are involved.

For Gary, he and Joani and the Alumni Connect mentors they recruit serve those who have already landed their first job post-college. The topics relate to many things such as the value of the work they have chosen once reality sets in. The biblical basis of vocation is another subject they discuss as this perspective gives real, significant, and eternal value to the alumni's day-to-day work. They also deal with relationship issues that are the norm for those leaving home and often with new marriages. Gary says that continuing to walk with God after they leave the close-knit college community along with many new responsibilities is a huge load for the younger people he is with. What he and their mentors seek to do is to build those deep heart relationships to help them learn to draw upon

God's strength and to experience His daily and ongoing presence in their lives. They can't go it alone.

Anne meets more with younger, mostly single people who are in the crucible of high stress Washington D.C. Many are newly arrived with all their roots having been pulled up. "They think they're going crazy, and sometimes they are. Either the work is too much, or their housing is terrible, or there's a relationship (colleague, romantic, roommate, etc.) that's killing them. Mostly they need me to listen and not be anxious, but ask them good questions; listen some more and tell them some occasional but relevant stories. Sometimes they're not even thinking of mentors when we start. I think they do long for one, but they don't imagine that anyone's really available." That's why she often takes the initiative and then tries to keep on meeting to build something deeper beyond initial problem solving.

When I talk to older people about mentoring, the question of duration usually comes up, so I asked these folks for their experience. The range was anywhere from once to a lifetime. How so? More formal arrangements that are part of a program generally last for the extent of that program. Everyone seemed to agree that other relationships of the more informal variety can last for years. As they grow older, the issues change and the relationship matures so that you will find you have a circle of younger friends to complement your older group. Occasionally putting some parts of that intergenerational mix together is a real winner, as B.J. and I have begun to find, at a table preferably. But mentoring usually has an end point. The norm seems to be informal as well, lives change, needs are realized, time together becomes less frequent, people move. Since it is informal, the ending or perhaps the dialing back becomes pretty evident.

We also talked briefly about what is called *reverse* mentoring. This is a relatively new phenomenon in the workplace, particularly because so many organizations are finding that their older workers are not nearly as sharp as their new hires at computer skills and understanding of the online world. In my leadership consulting practice, I began to see this as early as the late 90's and often wondered out loud to my clients how this would change things for them. Think about it. This is the first generation in the history of the world where the skills essential to doing daily work are taught by the young to the old. That dynamic must have consequences we don't fully understand, not the least being certain vocations skewing young as well as there being a more natural bent toward collaboration between generations. In the best sense, this can be a positive and in mentoring for life issues we all agreed it is. The negative side of what some feel is disdain by Millennials for their elders may be present in some organizations, but that's for someone else to parse. No one in our council discussion experienced this. On the contrary.

The benefits for the mentor are clearly there, even though we remind ourselves that is not our purpose. Yet, every one of these folks finds this a joy to have discovered how important this work is to young people—they are not seen as irrelevant. Each has come to see they are actually co-laboring with Christ in a role they have been prepared to fulfill. And, it's not a one-way street. Morna said that "Mentoring keeps me young and keeps me growing. I see God working in their lives, and it offers such hope!" Bruce has a slightly different take.

> *There are not many people whom I know that have gone as far in life as me and they generally do not understand what is going on with a person playing in the 4th quarter. The benefit I receive from my mentoring relationships is the knowledge that I've provided some influence into someone else's life who will follow my age group in leading others. The exception to this is my young student doctor and perhaps my grandson, also a student doctor. Their mentoring part generally has to do with where my health is in this stage of life.*

Anne added that she gets help in "technology, real estate

thinking, and new ideas for my own struggles with my adult children, as well as life in general."

I would add to the discussion that I think it's a good idea to
share prayer requests with the folks we mentor as they can then
take part in our life's concerns. Sometimes I ask them for their
feedback on teaching high school or things I'm writing (like this
book) for a reality check from a younger perspective. This is also
part of what is involved in becoming mature as a Christian that
I want them to experience—not just my speaking into their lives.

I often hear people demur, "I'm not sure I'd have anything to
say to someone younger. I'm still trying to figure out what I'm
going to do when I grow up!" I think we all agreed that you do not
need to be the Oracle at Delphi with answers to every problem
or issue the younger generations are facing. Remember that the
best of wisdom is not advice but a heart to heart communication,
one life to another, where you care, listen, pray, and share your
lives. Honestly, your stories of real life are treasures for someone
else whether they all have happy endings or not. Often people
also want to know if they are the only ones who hate their job, or
find marriage so hard, or can't understand why God doesn't just
do something about an intractable issue. Here is where your heart
of wisdom in knowing and trusting God in the darker places and
conundrums of life becomes invaluable.

We also talked together about the times when it is apparent
professional help is needed. As someone who has suffered from
depression more than once, I often can see where a recommenda-
tion for a good therapist is needed, and the same goes for marriage
issues that have deeper roots than B.J. and I can plumb. Usually a pastor has access to good people who can be trusted for
professional advice. The important takeaway in this part of the
conversation was this: in mentoring younger people, some things
are beyond the kind of wise, older friendship of a mentor, and
that will likely be apparent. Don't feel under a burden to do it all
or solve everything.

In closing our discussion, I asked the group whether they had any final words of wisdom to share about this role later in life. Here are a few gems.

Kay Hotaling said, "Don't ever think you have nothing to offer. Be authentic; trust God to use the real you. Confess that you are still in process yourself and you don't have all the answers." Morna agreed, by affirming the importance of humility and transparency:

> Can you 'lead with a limp?' I think to be a mentor, the mentor needs to be wisely vulnerable. No one wants to follow a perfect person, and none of us are perfect. It takes too much energy to project that image anyway, so find a way to be who you are, and to demonstrate in your relationship with the mentee how wonderful it is that God has created us each so uniquely, and uniquely for relationship with one another, and with Him. Encourage them to plunge into finding out more about what that means for them, too.

Gary particularly emphasized that the gift of being older has prepared you for this important role. Here is a guy in my own life that always encourages me on this road and evidences zeal for this vocation. He urges us to, "Do it!" For his work in searching for and pursuing individual mentors for younger people, he says to them, "I will lasso you and all of the years of life experience you have in the real world, seeing God work through it all, to pull you back from anyone putting you 'out to pasture' because you're 50, 60, 70, 80 years old! You have a *lot* to offer! They may not exactly know it, but a 22-year old is dying to hear what you have learned, and they will greatly benefit from your encouragement and all that can go on in building a healthy, proactive mentoring relationship." Now that's a great recruitment speech!

Nancy, Anne, and Bruce all agreed that for them the most important part of being a mentor is to listen. I'd add my "Amen" as well. Sometimes I can get too caught up in "telling and instruct-ing," maybe because I've spent so much time teaching, I get the roles confused, but they are right. I particularly like what Anne had to say, "Try very hard not to give direct advice, but to let them discover the advice with good questions or a story from your own experience. Never underestimate the power of story or of example."

You can see a wide variety of mentoring stories in our discussion. Whether the natural intergenerational community you engage with involves younger singles or marrieds, men or women, professional or personal concerns, for each of us there is a *gate* to sit by and younger people *passing by*. The nature of this later in life vocation may draw us toward a particular demographic, but as you can see here, the "fields are white for harvest." I think each member of this council would say, "if you haven't yet begun, you will love it once you do."

For B.J. and me, we have found that getting young couples ready for marriage has become a totally unexpected late in life joy as well as a place of special critical need, and the church is the place where they come beforehand.

MARRIAGE MENTORING

On preparing for marriage, we have come to appreciate Tolstoy's memorable words in Anna Karenina, "All happy families are alike; each unhappy family is unhappy in its own way." As he proceeds to tell the story of three families whose lives connect, he also describes three marriages in which happiness and unhappiness are played out with the final denouement of Anna's being to throw herself under the wheels of a train rather than live with her husband and her failures at marriage.[113] Along the way, the two other marriages Tolstoy describes have their challenges as well, and that's how we describe our own marriage. We sometimes even suggest *Anna Karenina* to couples as someone once did to us as a good read for those contemplating marriage or are in the very thick of it. It has not been all roses and pancakes, like many in our generation well know.

As we saw earlier, marriage remains under fire And the context differs from that of the elders when they were young. Regardless of those changes, we find all couples we mentor greatly desire to have a good, long marriage for life. They see even elders themselves continue to divorce at a much higher rate late in life than any generation before them, with their second and third marriages even more likely to fail. So, when B.J. and I considered possibly becoming marriage mentors to engaged couples in our church, we did so desiring to help these younger folks stay together, knowing from our own experience that it was a hard road.

Over ten years ago now, as members of mega church, we decided to try our hand. Part of our motivation was we felt like we needed to contribute, not just ingest ministry to us. Like many other large churches ours at the time was replete with programs for almost any situation, but marriage was a particular focus as the pastor and his wife, John and Susan Yates, were long-time speakers at national Family Life conferences. Now, twenty some younger couples later, we have found this to be one of the most satisfying things we have ever done, and most of all we love that we've been able to do it together as our church plant grows. That's an added incentive.

Unlike some of the other forms of mentoring, this one probably requires the most structure and preparation, but rest assured, the biggest preparation has been your married life. Most churches desire a time of preparation for marriage. As such, having marriage mentors is part of the deal for our church and trained mentors are needed.[116] For us, our preparation began with the older couple who ran the program meeting with us for four sessions, replicating what we would do afterward. The foundation for the conversations was a confidential inventory we each filled out separately called PRE-PARE/ENRICH©,[115] custom designed for those who are either dating or engaged (cohabiting or not), and married. Most people who are far smarter than me in marriage counseling believe this to be the best preparation available *when combined with mentoring*.

Suffice to say that we would probably not do pre-marriage mentoring without this information to work with. The track record of those using this inventory runs counter to the culture: their data says divorce rates are 30% lower for those who prepare this way.[116] What we like is that the inventory allows for substantive conversations together focusing on where the couple's perceptions may differ. It covers every important phase of marriage from communication to conflict resolution, from sex to money, expectations to family influences.

What B.J. and I normally do is begin by sharing their compared results on each general topic which then becomes the agenda as they sequentially discuss the places where they have differing perspectives. We let them talk to each other first, with us sitting by, about their responses, discussing what they each meant. This approach allows them to begin to practice communication and even conflict resolution. (BJ claims I even made one young bride-to-be cry, but I think it was stress.) More importantly they begin to learn better how to be transparent with each other on sometimes difficult topics. We generally will give them a few principles to use in having these conversations as they begin to learn about each other in some new ways. We also tell a few of our stories: good, bad, and often humorous. In these, we find we often return to Tim Keller's observation—"You always marry a stranger." In fact, we have found the best resource we have drawn on for this is Tim and Kathy Keller's *The Meaning of Marriage*.[117]

In this form of mentoring, our practice is to first meet them over coffee or brunch, usually after church, and get to know them a little to explain what we will be doing. Then for the four more structured sessions that follow we have a simple meal at our house where we begin by just talking and catching up, then we sit down with the inventory and a cup of coffee or some cookies and spend maybe an hour and a half or two hours going over two or three areas each time we meet.

What we particularly love is that over time so many of these younger couples have become our dear friends and we get the privilege of spending time with them later—together or one-on-one—when the realities of marriage roll out as they do for us all, particularly as new little lives enter the scene with their 24-7 demands. Preparing for marriage with a more experienced mentor couple and continuing to get together occasionally is a need in any church or in any neighborhood in America. This is one area we'd recommend exploring.

By now, if there was any mystery about the mentoring role of an elder, I hope these stories of both mentors and those who have been mentored give you the picture. But knowing human nature, many want it boiled down to some basic principles and practices. I've tried to do this cogently and with a minimalist view. My main reason for this philosophy is that this role of mentor is meant to be natural, not something requiring the certification of a license to practice. The bar is low. The need is high. The calling and power to contribute are compelling.

CHAPTER 9

SO WHAT AM I SUPPOSED TO DO...
AND NOT DO?

"A young man leaps and lands on an old man's legs."[118]

In a way, mentoring is an odd vocation. If you're like me, you will probably feel awkward even calling yourself a mentor and that's OK. It can sound presumptuous. This was underscored for me by Brooks, the young man wise beyond his years, whom I interviewed for this book in Chapter 7. Here is his cautionary. It's a good starting point to lead us into the one thing mentoring is *not*.

> *I think an explicit mentor-mentee relationship is an impediment to having or being a mentor. Like happiness, I think mentorship is something best achieved along the way. Injecting too much consciousness into the mentor-mentee dynamic could strip some honesty from the relationship as each party starts to think about the way a mentor or mentee should think or act, rather than interacting with each other as fellow travelers to the grave. This is not to say that such relationships cannot be engaged in consciously, even formally, but that there are some insidious hazards in doing so. We should ask ourselves questions:*
>
> *"Why do I want to be a mentor?"*
> *"Is there some element of personal aggrandizement in being a mentor, to think of oneself as a teacher, a molder of another?"*
> *"Why do I want to have a mentor?"*

"Is it to get something from that mentor, to use the mentor to achieve some goal, to manage his opinion of me?"

This hand-wringing over the intentionality of mentor-mentee relationships is no doubt unjust to the good people mentoring and being mentored in the world, but Uncle Screwtape is clever.

It's Not about You

If there is one fundamental negative principle to begin with, it is that you do not take this role on for the purpose of acclaim ("Aren't I great to spend time with young people?") or for the purpose of being in charge of shaping another person's life ("Without me, she would not have become a writer.") or as a feel-good end in itself. It's not about you—and maybe that is a relief. Let it also be a watchword. It's in the doing, not in the title.

I remember the very first young man I mentored. I only realized I had done so in retrospect a couple of years after we began when his wife thanked me using that very term. At the time, I was managing a large organization change effort and he was a young consultant that was part of a team we had engaged from a big firm to help with the IT side of the transformation. I was learning a lot about the difficult nature of change, learning how to transform not only processes but hearts, minds, and organization culture. I was reading a ton, talking to wiser people, and found it both exhilarating and a bit of a scary high wire act. But the numerous textbooks and journal articles I read did not anywhere near prepare me for executing the real thing. It was a tough yet good school of daily learning. I was in no position to think I knew much at all, let alone to be able to mentor someone, a word hardly yet in my vocabulary.

Somehow this young guy thought I had experienced something that would help his consulting career. We began having breakfast once a week or so, bouncing ideas off of each other. In the process I learned we attended the same church and had not even known it. In time we went well beyond sharing our thoughts about organization change as we talked of career paths, family challenges, and spiritual

116

issues. I also slowly began to realize he thought of me as wiser, not just older, and I also noticed this was a subtle opportunity for pride which began to creep in. To this day, I find I must remind myself of my purpose when mentoring and go back to why God has me here: it is not about me, it's about my Father, about someone else, not for any supposed glory. That is where you start.

To Begin

In what follows, I am drawing upon my experience and that of our wise council to identify just a few basics. As we have seen, there is no "formula" to beginning a mentoring relationship other than to have a mutually recognized connection. Look for that in the two places where intergenerational relationships are normal—work and church. If you are in your retirement years then it is church, probably the best ground for beginning.

In my experience, it can begin with a simple conversation at any gathering, formal or informal. Sometimes when I speak I will connect with someone in the audience afterward. Other times a casual conversation in an odd moment opens up an obvious need and a more extended follow-up is natural. Even an arrangement to get together by a third party can be helpful—if it is not felt as obligatory. It can be as simple as saying "Hey, would you like to grab coffee sometime and talk more on this?" like Anne uses. If you are younger, the same applies—don't be reluctant to ask.

Even then, there may be only a single conversation, or a sporadic connection, or it could be something that may continue regularly for months, even years. Don't pressure yourself into some norm that does not exist.

It's Their Agenda, Not Yours

In general, there is going to be a purpose for getting together, at least in the beginning—it is *theirs*, even if you initiate the get-together. It can be formalized, as we have seen, but usually the topics will begin to emerge more from a neutral, "How's your week gone?"

117

type of conversation. Of course, once you have spent some time together, there may well be a regular topic each time: e.g., fighting temptations to lust, anger at a toxic boss, or tensions at home. What can be challenging, I find, is the realization that many younger people have so much to learn and of course I could simply tell them—and so I too often do so as I've already confessed. Bad idea.

Granted, lectures about what you have found is important for a life well-lived are of some value, but be patient; this will come out all in due time if needed. Asking questions, listening patiently without interruption (no harm in repeating that), expressing caring, then maybe sharing a comparable story—this balance is of far greater worth to the other person than simply lecturing, especially for Millennials. We are building heart relationships, not running a live search engine. We are getting together to meet their needs; that is Job #1. But to discover what these needs are takes restraint and patience for trust to build to the point of greater transparency. Sometimes good questions are helpful.

Often what I find is that the person I am meeting with saves the hardest issue for last, "Oh, just one more thing." Sometimes you can sense this, but sometimes it simply comes out of the blue. If you have already broached some tough issues on previous occasions, then follow-up is more comfortable, especially on often sensitive topics like pornography, wrongful attraction, or ethical issues at work. But don't be surprised that issues emerge that are surprising to you.

This is not to say the conversation is one-sided, like a Freudian therapist who nods, "um-hum, please continue," every few minutes. Rather, it is good if you have similar stories to share from time to time concerning when you were their age, especially if you learned from a mistake, or a time when you and your wife encountered something similar and it was tough to resolve. Stories of what you have seen in the raising of your kids are always needed for baffled newer parents. Keep in mind, in a postmodern culture, stories, not doctrine, are held in high regard.

As discussed earlier, do not be reluctant to appropriately share your life at times, personal prayer needs, and sometimes our own challenges, but for the most part I save those for my close friends or my small group as that is not the main purpose here. I know I am not on the road to sainthood so I don't want to convey that sense either. Stories of where I learned, perhaps from my failures, are the most helpful it seems to me. You'll get the feel of it. Live into it. Here is one way to begin.

Tell Your Big Story

When it comes to telling stories, here is an idea I picked up from Rick Woolworth. When he and I first began discussing what both of us were about in our work with the next generation, he asked if we could pause a bit and tell each other our life stories. He took notes, and later I did the same with him. What I have come to like about this approach is we get a pretty complete picture in one narrative of place, parents, key relationships, career trajectory, shaping events, beliefs, etc. Stories connect the dots; while vignettes, or answers to questions, or tackling issues are more akin to bullet points, but without context. Eventually, we might begin to make the connections or fill in the gaps, but I agree with Rick—a life narrative in some form is a far better place to start if possible.

Then there are good questions.

Four Big Questions

From past experience, there are at least four big questions, the branches from which all other issues seem to flow—for younger people at least. If these places are not touched on in our storytelling or early conversations, I have found it is usually good to begin to ask one of these to draw the person out and to deepen our relationship. These are personal, they can even have some pain involved, but developing a more transparent, trusting relationship means discussing these somewhere along to road of our time together, though not all in one sitting of course. They can usually be asked while addressing something on their agenda.

The first question is foundational, it concerns their parents and upbringing. I particularly want to understand what kind of relationship the person had with their father[119] as that so often shapes how a person sees God. I also want to see how the person related to their mother, a particularly telling relationship for both relationships and marriage. This insight gives me a window into other questions and possible issues. This is not intended to be a probing, psychological inquiry, just an open-ended question such as "What was your dad like?" "How does your mom like your new girlfriend/wife?" Or, "How did your family spend their evenings/vacations/holidays?" For younger people who have left home, there almost always are unresolved issues with mom and/or dad.

It's also helpful to understand how the parents got along with each other during the growing up years. Their example often shapes dating choices and patterns as well as decisions on delaying or entering into marriage, though they can be unseen.

What I eventually hope to hear more about is an answer to, "What is your relationship like now with your folks?" Is there a need for forgiveness? Has the relationship matured to being more that of friends than parents who must control the scene? Does the person seek the counsel of his parents and trust their insights? Or, are they having to take on responsibility for their parents in some way?

If married, how do her parents treat the spouse and the spouse's family? Are they still involved in their lives in a good way? Basically, as they talk about this key relationship, I am looking for whether the person can, indeed, honor their parents in their older years, and whether they have been able to *leave and cleave* if they are married, or have *left home* if they are single. Is lack of forgiveness on either side haunting them? If these relationship tensions are unresolved, it may well be an accident waiting to happen—or one where the wreckage is still being poked over. The main thing we can do together in the growing relationship is to understand how critical our relationship with our parents is in shaping who we are, no matter our age. As someone who is of their parents' generation

SO WHAT AM I SUPPOSED TO DO...

(or older), as the council reflected on, we can offer something easier to hear than parental voices. That's biblical truth, not just psychology.

Second, I want to know about why they came to be in this place always a critical decision, particularly for a town such as Washington, D.C. Like many big cities, this is typically a transitory spot—often a stop on the way to somewhere else. For D.C., it is a place where the coin of the realm is power. Most come here for a job, but then they realize it is far more than that, it is a culture all its own. This is not so much a conversation about the nation's capital as it is about the shaping role of place in our lives—something that lies beneath the surface in forming who we are, as the stories of Israel tell us repeatedly. Most people do not grow up in a culture where power or access to power, one of the three *gods* that remain in the high places of America, (the others being sex and money), reigns. If a young person is a newcomer, I want to help them see a little about how this odd company town works; that it has its traps as well as its plausibility structure that most people adhere to, usually unconsciously. We older people understand these things, having lived here for a time and put roots down deep. Younger people often have not.

The third question is related—how do they understand their vocation (if they even do)—their calling and preparation by God for doing the work they are doing and for building the life they are forming? It is really a question that helps uncover their *telos*, their purpose for all of life, and whether their faith connects with this vocation seamlessly or whether they have little to do with each other. What gets each one of us out of bed almost every morning, how we spend our time on this earth, and how we wrestle with some principled balance in a hectic world matters to us—but I hope to help them see it matters to God. Many young people fear they *got it wrong*, or they are stuck and fear God is disappointed or absent.

What I often find is that many (not all) young people begin with a dream, but soon come to conclude that their secular work has little

121

purpose beyond a paycheck and a lifestyle. That their work *really* matters to God in extending God's kingdom into every corner is often lost in the struggle to make their way in the world. I want to be sure to ask at some point whether they can see that what they do each day pleases God or whether they pine for something more meaningful, a sense of purpose they yearn for. The single, emerging adult scene is too often one of *amusing ourselves to death*[120] as Christian Smith uncovered. This can eventually lead to cynicism without a solid life perspective. Every key metropolitan area, like Washington, has its particular cultural characteristics, and an older, more experienced adult can help translate these and make a huge difference in helping a younger person to navigate the uncertain shoals toward more meaningful relationships and activities and some peace about their calling.

Finally, a fourth question is, what are their most important relationships like? Since marrying later is now the norm, relationships loom large in their lives. Here is where the world has changed so much from my era to the Millennials' as observed earlier. In cities where young workers come and go so often, places like DC, LA, Denver, New York, Atlanta, etc., this new lifestyle makes things more complicated than most of what we elders have known. Millennials often have something more akin to a tribe rather than a couple of best friends. Yet, a lot of younger people are not only looking for someone to just "hang out" with, as they say; they are often looking for a community, a neighborhood to live in, and sometimes a good church, and something romantic, too. The online life many are finding leaves an unmet hunger for real connections, though dating is mediated online more often than ever.

The transition from college to career to adult life is not simple, nor is it fast, and those relatively new to a city can find it lonely. What a good mentor can do is to help make those human connections within a church if they are not in one, to a good small group or to a community of solid people—other adults, younger or older, who can be of help.

For singles, the culture of modern sexuality that exists so pervasively is not just in sitcoms. It is always present and is common in the neighborhoods where singles flock. I have had to learn to ask more direct (but respectful) questions at times about relationships, and to expect more direct answers on sexuality or damage from past encounters. Christian singles are not immune to these pressures by any means. Pornography is always on the table with the young men I come to know well. I've learned to ask, "So how are you doing with pornography?" if it doesn't come up after a while. It is pervasive, sad to say.

For younger marrieds, the question of relationships lie more in how they are growing their marriage in the midst of a culture that values marriage less and less. They need to be with older married couples who can share their lives and affirm their good choices when the speed bumps appear.

Of course, these questions are just the beginning of areas to explore, but how parents, place, vocation, and relationships have shaped and continue to shape people, I have found, continue to be where most issues arise in mentoring discussions, but each has their relationship with God as the foundational one. Are their loves and desires rightly ordered? This is what is most important to spend time on together.

The Question beneath All Questions

Underlying each of these four questions is the most fundamental one of all for each person. Our God is a purposeful God and above all he has created us, as John Stott says, for the purpose of being conformed to the image of his Son, becoming like Jesus.[121] Hence, the relationships we have with the people who formed us from birth, the place and the work where we are called to bear fruit, and the community of relationships within which we are called to live out our lives—married or single—all are part of God's process of shaping us within this crucible of a fallen, yet redeemed, world. What a person's relationship is with their Creator, Savior, and

Friend is the question whose answer matters most, and we want to work on that together as much as possible. For some of us, using Jesus in a complete sentence is more awkward than talking about the weather or our favorite restaurant. I've found speaking of my relationship with my Lord takes practice in speaking simply and without religiously stilted language.

If you are to be an elder at the gate for the next generations, God has called you together into this relationship for the purpose of mutual sanctification, becoming more like Jesus. I count on that truth for assurance, a truth he has established long ago to be carried out as one generation succeeds the next. It is the work of God's Spirit to do this work in us, but it is his design, as we have seen, that one generation reaches back to the next for their benefit. We must speak the truth in love and sometime discuss the deeper question of, "How are you and the Lord doing in your relationship?"—and, of course, to share your own journey honestly alongside, not from a pulpit of superiority or judgment, but in a heart-to-heart manner, not head-to-head. "Are you spending good time together with the Lord?" "Are you getting to know him better?" "What do you think he thinks about all this we've been talking about in your life?" These are the kind of regular questions that are meat for conversation each time, as your relationship deepens. Be aware also that the other person may feel a little awkward so keep it light and casual using your own expression as an example.

Asking clearer questions that probe deeper toward the heart than, "How is your spiritual life going?" or, "Have you been going to church?" helps us to elicit the places where we can be co-laborers with God in the formation of maturity in a younger person. Such deeper conversations also give us a better understanding of how we can pray for them—perhaps our most critical, yet unappreciated task in helping one another. As mentors, we want to get to the heart, not simply the behavior, whenever we can. If someone knows you are truly praying for them, and if you are regularly asking them how you can pray and how they are progressing, you are telling them you care, that you think about them far more than just when you're across the table or walking on the hiking path. Then ask them later about what you have prayed for, but also be sure to ask them to pray for you.

CONVERSATIONS OF CONSEQUENCE

Steve Garber, someone I have learned so much from, has been a mentor to hundreds of young people over the years, and is a good and dear friend. He often says that our aim as mentors of those coming after is to have *conversations of consequence*. What he means by this is that we use our waning time on earth to discuss the important questions of life together with younger people; that we are actually meant and made to do so at this stage of life. We know what their issues are for having passed through those years. We generally know the right questions to ask by our own experiences. Thus, below surface consequential conversations, week after week, are where we can contribute in ways no one else really can. That's actually the plan!

Finally, and perhaps this is gratuitous, but a conversation of consequence in our age does not need a distracting third entity. If you are going to care about the person you're with, I have decided it means leaving the mobile device in the car or shutting it off and keeping it out of sight, not setting the little rectangular box on the table or park bench, where it may audibly buzz. I don't need to bring it out as an arbitrator to resolve questions, or as a fact checker, or as a source of overcoming short-term memory loss, or as a reminder we are out of time.

KAIROS OR CHRONOS?

We discussed earlier that the importance of time, given as a gift to others, is highly valued by those who are younger. It is the one completely non-renewable resource placed at the disposal of each person on earth and we become more aware as we grow older that time is fleeting, seeming to pass more quickly than when we

125

were younger, like the sands in an hour glass. That is *chronos* time, the Greek word that gives us a perspective of time as minutes and seconds and agendas and calendars. But there is another way to think about time.

When Paul instructs us to, "Look carefully then how you walk, not as unwise but as wise, making the best use of the time, because the days are evil,"[122] the word he uses is not chronos, but *kairos*. This view of time is that of an opportune moment or a due season. Living as elders at the gate, mentors to the next generations, means not simply being wise, as if we were dispensers of Wikipedia articles, but as *living wisely*, continuing to gain hearts of wisdom as God intends up until the end.

We thus need to make room in our lives for such growth and for the possibilities he brings by us at our gate, not to let chronos drive out kairos. As older people, retired or not, we are not only still busy with our own concerns, but we are constantly being pulled between the joys and sorrows of life in a world and a culture that is not simply secular, but is antithetical to the Christian story, filling up our time with tweets and dings and to-do's and bucket lists. How often do you hear someone who is retired say, "I am busier than ever." Sometimes we want the path of least resistance where we can go more gently with people our own age and make the early bird special, binge a video series, or go early to bed. But I hope by now it's clear that there is more that God has planned for our days.

We are not only needed, but no one else can do what we elders can do and are created to do, face-to-face. Neither Google, YouTube, Instagram, or self-help videos can substitute for what one generation can give as a gift to another. The practice of mentoring is a countercultural use of precious time. In a *chronos* world we can be the *kairos* people. A good conversation of consequence takes time, unhurried time, preferably time experienced in a leisurely way; for this, the ancients understood, was the basis for a strong civilization.[123] This is not just one more meeting or another interview to cram into a busy schedule.

126

Enough said. I don't want to be a grumpy, old man.

Well, actually, there is more, but I am duly warned, as you should be, to "Be careful, for writing books is endless, and much study wears you out."[124] Save your energy for the real thing. It's time to end this narrative and get to the gate.

CHAPTER 10

GIVING YOURSELF AWAY TO THE VERY END

O God, from my youth you have taught me, and I still proclaim
your wondrous deeds. So even to old age and gray hairs, O God, do
not forsake me, until I proclaim your might to another generation,
your power to all those to come.[125]

For many years, Wendell Berry, the essayist, novelist, and poet has been quietly at work on Sundays writing personal poetry to reflect on his life, and on creation, and the Creator while he rests from the week. In a small volume, some of these musings are recorded to be read to oneself, he says, more than at a public reading. As far as I know, he continues this practice. Looking through these chronologically, I was struck that as he grew older, more of his thoughts seemed to turn to the questions of the last part of life, to being an elder, turning it over in his mind. One reflection I have particularly come to love more each time I read it helps me think about how to live out this time of life right to the end.

> *No, no there is no going back.*
> *Less and less you are*
> *that possibility you were.*
> *More and more you have become*
> *those lives and deaths*
> *that have belonged to you.*
> *You have become a sort of grave*

containing much that was
and is no more in time, beloved,
then, now, and always.
And so you have become a sort of tree
standing over a grave.
Now more than ever you can be
generous toward each day
that comes, young, to disappear
forever and yet remain
unaging in the mind.
Every day you have less reason not to give yourself away.[126]

What I hear Berry saying to himself and to us is that as we grow older we must come to grips with the reality that we simply cannot go back to our youth or middle age. Here, the metaphors he selects are telling: "a sort of grave"—"a sort of tree." The dreams that lay as possibilities in our youth and even the hopes have to die. What we experienced in strong, supple bodies cannot be endlessly replayed like a videorecorder. Yet we can say that when we leave this behind, we can then find that what is left becomes rich compost for the wisdom for our older self that slowly grows alongside and within our aging bodies. What gently emerges can be something unexpected, perhaps even more meaningful than our younger minds and spirits could have grasped. We can age with confidence and purpose if we have eyes to see what has gone before and what has been intended for us from the beginning, all as part of our story written long ago.

Rather than lament lost youth, or while away our last years in ease, we can instead live life with more generosity. We have even less reason not to give ourselves away to others as we grow older; not to follow the siren call of our culture's bucket list ending. In just these few words, this sage poet captures what I have been struggling to convey on these pages.

We each know that as time passes we have and will continue

to experience the deaths of the lives that nurtured ours—parents, teachers, pastors, friends, and mentors. But as we live on, we draw strength unbidden from those lives that came before ours, and from God, who answers our prayer that we have the *kairos* to declare his might to the next generation.

In what is entitled by the psalmist as a song or poem for the Sabbath, like Berry he reflects on the end of life:

> *The righteous flourish like the palm tree*
> *and grow like a cedar in Lebanon.*
> *They are planted in the house of the Lord;*
> *they flourish in the courts of our God. They still bear*
> *fruit in old age;*
> *they are ever full of sap and green,*
> *to declare that the Lord is upright;*
> *he is my rock, and there is no unrighteousness in him.*[127]

We can find we bear new and delightful fruit in our maturing years, even in old age, far beyond what we may have imagined in our younger days. When we give our lives to others who pass by the gate, we can be confident that they will one day nurture those that come behind them. Thus, our legacy lives on, not in monuments to ourselves, but in the generations that follow ours, just as they were designed to do from the very first. It is then we can rightly say, "Not to us, O Lord, not to us, but to your name give glory, for the sake of your steadfast love and your faithfulness!"[128]

THE BEST IS YET TO BE

Probably 30 years ago now, about the time I had the distinct sense I was growing older in that "Sir" moment I described earlier, I had a gift-dilemma. I am always lame on giving gifts to B.J., so I had this bright idea that for our anniversary I would have a calligrapher write a portion of a poem I had recently discovered and then have it framed. I think she really liked it as it still hangs on her office wall beside her desk. (I'd tell you the waffle-maker first year anniversary gift story and my mother in law's acerbic comment, but there's not enough space. Sorry.)

I can look back now and say I had as yet no fully formed idea of what I was even thinking about when I gave her that as a gift. It was tough to put my now 75-year old head on that 45-year old body. At the time what the poem expressed for me was a sort of yearning that we would one day see good fruit come to bear, despite our too young marriage, the challenging days of raising children in workaholic Washington, a painful separation, and just how hard it all was at times. I knew I wanted to do better as a husband, father, child of God, and friend—and was painfully aware of how short I fell. I didn't really like the guy in the mirror all that well, but I had hopes that together, with God, we could look forward to better days. What I didn't realize then was that I did not appreciate what truth lay here. As the poem says so succinctly, "the best is yet to be," just the way God planned and wrote the story, in this life and also in the new heaven and the new earth. He redeemed, but he also restored, and is restoring in ways I could not have anticipated. As we end, I want to share this as both a vision and as a reinforcement of all that has gone before in our discussion—for it is true.

> *Grow old along with me!*
> *The best is yet to be,*
> *The last of life, for which the first was made:*
> *Our times are in His hand*
> *Who saith "A whole I planned,*
> *Youth shows but half; trust God: see all, nor be afraid!"*[129]

1. "Everything is Broken," Bob Dylan, (Special Rider Music1989).
2. Proverbs 1:24-26, ESV
3. The term "emerging adult" is a relatively new sociological term that will be used throughout to designate those who are roughly between 18 and 30. It describes the phenomenon of our times that there is an extended period between adolescence and full adulthood.
4. For our purposes, Millennials are that generation born after 1980, ending approximately 1996 when the next (Generation Z) begins. Millennials: A Portrait of Generation Next; Confident. Connected. Open to Change., Pew Research Center, 2010, 4.
5. Urban Dictionary, Adulting (v): to do grown up things and hold responsibilities such as, a 9-5 job, a mortgage/rent, a car payment, or anything else that makes one think of grown-ups. Accessed July 20, 2018, https://www.urbandictionary.com/define.php?term=Adulting.
6. The term "third third" will be used throughout to designate a somewhat imprecise time period, the last phase of life after the primary career has ended. It is drawn from Walter C. Wright, The Third Third of Life: Preparing for you Future, (Downers Grove, IL: Intervarsity Press, 2012). This is an excellent guide in eight sessions of readings and self-reflection to prepare for the road ahead. Highly recommended.
7. Dylan Thomas, Do Not Go Gentle Into that Good Night, Poets.org, https://www.poets.org/poetsorg/poem/do-not-go-gentle-good-night, accessed August 10, 2016.
8. Ralph Waldo Emerson, Self-Reliance and Other Essays: Series I and II, (Seahorse Classics, 2011), 189
9. Psalm 90:12, ESV
10. Ernest Becker, The Denial of Death, (New York: Simon and Schuster, 1973)
11. Leo Tolstoy, Two Old Men, (McLean, VA: The Trinity Forum, 1994).
12. Ibid., 31.
13. Ibid., 33
14. Soren Kierkegaard, Quora, https://www.quora.com/How-do-you-interpret-S%C3%B8ren-Kierkegaards-view-that-%E2%80%9CLife-can-only-be-understood-backwards-but-it-must-be-lived-forwards-%E2%80%9D, accessed April 14, 2018.

15. Richard Leider, The Power of Purpose, (San Francisco: Berrett-Koehler Publishers, 1996)
16. II Timothy 4:7, ESV
17. Portions of this first appeared as The Last Lap: Vocation for the Elderly, Washington Institute for Faith, Vocation and Culture website, http://www.washingtoninst.org/7665/the-last-lap-vocation-for-the-elderly/, March 19, 2014.
18. Psalm 92:10-11, ESV.
19. J.I. Packer, Finishing Our Course with Joy: Guidance from God for Engaging with our Aging, (Wheaton, IL: Crossway, 2014),
20. Ibid
21. Packer is referring here to Isaiah 40:29-31: "He gives power to the faint, and to him who has no might he increases strength. Even youths shall faint and be weary, and young men shall fall exhausted; but they who wait for the Lord shall renew their strength; they shall mount up with wings like eagles; they shall run and not be weary; they shall walk and not faint."
22. Philippians 3:8-10, ESV
23. II Timothy 4:7, ESV.
24. Dr, J. Robert Clinton, The Making of a Leader: Recognizing The Lessons and Stages of Leadership Development, (Colorado Springs: NavPress, 2012)
25. Dr. J. Robert Clinton, Clinton Biblical Leadership Commentary.
26. Atul Gawande, Being Mortal: Medicine and What Matters in the End, (New York: Henry Holt and Company, 2014).
27. Marcus Tullius Cicero, Ethical Writings of Cicero II, Cicero De Senectute (On Old Age), Online Library of Liberty, http://oll.libertyfund.org/titles/cicero-on-old-age-de-senectute, accessed July 22, 2018.
28. 2 Corinthians 4:16-18, ESV
29. The title for this chapter and the discussion that follows in the first part, is drawn primarily from the extensive research by Jean M. Twenge, published in Generation Me: Why Today's Young Americans Are More Confident, Assertive, Entitled—and More Miserable Than Ever Before, (New York: Simon and Schuster, 2014) and from iGen: Why Today's Super-Connected Kids Are Growing Up Less Rebellious, More Tolerant, Less Happy—and Completely Unprepared for Adulthood, (New York: Simon and Schuster, 2017).
30. "Kids," lyrics by Lee Adams and Charles Strause, from Bye Bye Birdie, original movie soundtrack, March 29, 1963
31. "The Millenials are Coming," Johns Hopkins Department of Pathology, 2018.
32. Daniel Brea, Job Interview, https://vimeo.com/239050403/239050403, accessed December 2, 2017, 2:00 pm.

33. The actual quote is "Houston we've had a problem here," uttered by Jack Swigert and then repeated at the request of the Houston controllers by Jim Lovell, the Commander of the Shuttle.
34. Twenge, 31, though for part of the Boomers youth the draft was in place.
35. The material that follows was drawn largely from my thesis for a Masters in Theological Studies, An Old Solution to a Modern Problem: Classical Education and the Crisis of Faith in the Millennials, (Washington, D.C.: Wesley Theological Seminary, 2014).
36. "Madison" is a fictional student, a composite of characteristics seen among several of my students over the years.
37. "Nones" on the Rise: One in Five Adults Have No Religious Affiliation, (Washington, DC: The Pew Research Center's Forum on Religion and Public Life, 2012)
38. Ibid., 10.
39. To date, the NSYR's primary research findings have been published in three volumes: Soul Searching: The Religious and Spiritual Lives of American Teenagers; Souls in Transition: The Religious and Spiritual Lives of Emerging Adults; and Lost in Transition: The Dark Side of Emerging Adulthood. Christian Smith has been the lead author on all three volumes. (New York: Oxford University Press, 2005, 2009, and 2011, respectively).
40. This overall summary was provided by one of the primary researchers assisting Christian Smith, Kenda Creasy Dean, in her own book, Almost Christian: What the Faith of Our Teenagers is Telling the American Church, (New York: Oxford University Press, 2010), 17-21.
41. Ephesians 4:15, ESV
42. Christian Smith, Soul Searching, 262
43. Richard Fry, For First Time in Modern Era, Living With Parents Edges Out Other Living Arrangements for 18- to 34-Year-Olds, Washington, D.C.: Pew Research Center, May 2016.
44. Christian Smith, Souls in Transition, 6.
45. Christian Smith with Karl Christofferson, Hilary Davidson, and Patricia Snell Herzog, Lost in Transition: The Dark Side of Emerging Adulthood, (New York: Oxford University Press, 2011).
46. Boudleaux Bryant, Felice Bryant, Raining in My Heart, Lyrics © House of Bryant Publications, 1957.
47. Tyler Joseph, Stressed Out, © Warner-Tamerlane Publishing Corp.
48. Twenge, 145.
49. Ibid., 146.
50. Jean Twenge, "Have Smartphones Destroyed a Generation?" Atlantic, September 2017.
51. Romans 2:1-3, ESV

52. Psalm 78:4-8, ESV
53. Tom Wolfe, "The 'Me' Decade and the Third Great Awakening," New York Magazine, August 23, 1976, http://nymag.com/news/features/45938/, accessed June 23, 2016.
54. Christian Smith, Soul Searching, 171.
55. Chad Barlow, Putting Away Childish Things: C.S. Lewis on Immaturity in an Age of Emerging Adulthood, unpublished paper, Wycliffe College, Oxford University, 2013, 7.
56. Thomas E. Bergler, "When Are We Going to Grow Up? The Juvenilization of American Christianity," Christianity Today, June 8, 2012. http://www.christianitytoday.com/ct/2012/june/when-are-we-going-to-grow-up.html, accessed January 28, 2014.
57. Ibid.
58. Ibid.
59. Ibid.
60. Tom Wolfe, Ibid.
61. Jean M. Twenge, Generation Me: Why Today's Young Americans Are More Confident, Assertive, Entitled--and More Miserable Than Ever Before, (New York: Atria Books, 2014), 61.
62. Love to Know, Historical Divorce Rate Statistics, http://divorce.lovetoknow.com/Historical_Divorce_Rate_Statistics. Accessed July 1, 2016.
63. W. Bradford Wilcox, "The Evolution of Divorce," National Affairs, Fall 2009, https://www.nationalaffairs.com/publications/detail/the-evolution-of-divorce, accessed December 2, 2017, 3:10 pm.
64. Ibid.
65. David Brooks, Bobos in Paradise: The New Upper Class and How They Got There, (New York: Simon and Schuster, 2001), 9.
66. Chap Clark, Hurt 2.0: Inside the World of Today's Teenagers (Grand Rapids: Baer Academic, 2004, 2011),viii.
67. Ibid., 15.
68. Ibid., 23.
69. Daniel, J. Siegel, Brainstorm: The Power and Purpose of the Teenage Brain, (New York: Jeremy P. Tarcher/Penguin,
70. Robert Putnam, Bowling Alone : The Collapse and Revival of American Community, (New York: Simon and Schuster, 2001). Identifies the loss of community in the last 40+ years as arising from the time pressures of commuting, work, television watching, and to financial pressures which have led to both parents having to work.
71. Holly B. Shakya and Nicholas A. Christakis, "Association of Facebook Use With Compromised Well-Being: A Longitudinal Study," American Journal of Epidemiology, Volume 85, Issue 3, February 2017.
72. See Robert Bellah, et al, Habits of the Heart: Individualism and

Commitment in American Life, (Berkeley: University of California Press, 1989), for perhaps the best explication of the rise of individualism and the therapeutic in America and its possible implications for community and social capital.

73. Chap Clark, 27.
74. Ibid.
75. David Elkind. The Hurried Child: Growing Up Too Fast, Too Soon,(Reading, MA: Addison-Wesley, 1st Ed.—1981; 2nd Ed.—1994; 3rd Ed.—2001).
76. Clark, 30-31.
77. Ibid., 35.
78. Ibid., 60.
79. Patricia Hersh, A Tribe Apart: A Journey into the Heart of American Adolescence, (New York: Ballantine Books, 1998).
80. Clark, 34.
81. Merriam Webster Dictionary online, "Words We're Watching," https://www.merriam- webster.com/words-at-play/adulting, accessed December 2, 2017, 4:00 pm.
82. Proverbs 22:6, ESV.
83. Deuteronomy 4:9, ESV
84. Deuteronomy 6:4-7, ESV
85. Proverbs 22:6, ESV
86. Max De Pree, transcript of interview, De Pree Mentoring Conference, Max De Pree Center for Leadership, Pasadena, CA, October 18, 2002, as cited in Walter C. Wright, 101.
87. Exemplary Youth Ministry Study, www.exemplarym.org accessed December 18, 2013.
88. Derek Melleby interview of David Sertran, co-author of Spiritual Formation in Emerging Adulthood: A Practical Theology for College and Young Adult Ministry appearing in The College Initiative online newsletter, accessed July 28, 2018, https://cpyu.org/
89. Vern L. Bengston, Families and Faith: How Religion is Passed Down Across Generations, (New York: Oxford University Press, 2013).
90. Amy Ziettlow, interview conducted with Vern Bengston, Christianity Today, "Religion Runs in the Family," September 20, 2013, http://www.christianitytoday.com/ct/2013/august-web-only/religion-runs-in-family.html, accessed January 7, 2013.
91. Ibid.
92. Galatians 1:6-9, ESV
93. Kenda Creasy Dean, 11.
94. Ibid., 72.
95. Ibid.

96. Steve Garber, Fabric of Faithfulness: Weaving Together Belief and Behavior, (Downers Grove, IL: IVP Books, 2nd Revised edition, 2007).

97. Ray Blunt, "From the Head of Zeus: How Leaders Are Really Grown," Comment Magazine, June 18, 2010.

98. Lester J. Cappon, ed., The Adams-Jefferson Letters (Chapel Hill: The University of North Carolina Press, 1959), 384.

99. Mark 10:42-45, ESV

100. Psalm 139:16, ESV—"Your eyes saw my unformed substance; in your book were written, every one of them, the days that were formed for me, when as yet there was none of them."

101. Deuteronomy 21:18-20, ESV

102. Peggy Noonan, "Welcome Back Duke," The Wall Street Journal, October 12, 2001.

103. Perhaps the most recent of these is Rod Drehrer's The Benedict Option: A Strategy for Christians in a Post-Christian Nation, 2016.

104. Taken from Ray Blunt, Crossed Lives – Crossed Purposes: Why Thomas Jefferson Failed and William Wilberforce Persisted in Leading an End to Slavery, (Eugene, OR: Wipf and Stock Publishers, 2012).

105. Alumni Connect: http://www.establishalumni.com/

106. The Fellows Initiative: https://www.thefellowsinitiative.org/

107. Nav20s: http://nav20s.org/

108. Officers Christian Fellowship: http://www.ocfusa.org/

109. Growing and Building: http://growingandbuilding.com/

110. Young Life: https://www.younglife.org/Pages/default.aspx

111. Telemachus Network: http://telemachusnetwork.org/

112. C. S. Lewis Fellows Program: http://www.cslewisinstitute.org/Fellows_Program

113. http://nancyzieglerpaintings.com/wordpress/

114. Leo Tolstoy, Anna Karenina, (New York: Penguin Books, 2001)

115. https://www.prepare-enrich.com

116. Ibid.

117. David H. Olson, Amy K. Olson, and Peter J. Larson, Journal of Family & Community Ministries, "PREPARE-ENRICH Program: Overview and New Discoveries about Couples," 25: 2012, 30-44.

118. Tim and Kathy Keller, The Meaning of Marriage: Facing the Complexities of Commitment with the Wisdom of God, (New York: Penguin Books, 2013).

119. Wendell Berry, A Timbered Choir: The Sabbath Poems, 1979-1997, Washington, D.C.: Counterpoint, 1998), 161

120. I also owe Dr. Jim Houston a mention here as this was one of the first questions he asked me after we first met. I soon learned that this is a standard question of his that he believes tells more about a person than anything other than whether they are in Christ or not.

121. A term coined by Neil Postman in his now classic book by the same name.

122. John Stott's Final Sermon: The Model - Becoming More Like Christ, The Keswick Convention, July 17, 2007.

123. Ephesians 5:15-17, ESV

124. See Josef Pieper, Leisure: The Basis of Culture, (Carmel, IN: Liberty Fund, 1999).

125. Ecclesiastes 12:12, New Living Translation

126. Psalm 71:17-18, ESV

127. Berry, 167.

128. Psalm 92:12-15, ESV

129. Psalm 115:1, ESV

130. Robert Browning, from "Rabbi Ben Ezra," in Poetry for Pleasure, (Garden City, NY: Doubleday & Company, Inc., 1960), 184.

Acknowledgments

It is a good custom to say thank you, especially when it is not gratuitous politeness but a heartfelt expression that still seems somehow inadequate. That's how I feel at the end of a long process of trying to tell a decent story about elders as mentors knowing all the people who contributed to my life and to the writing of this book.

If I think back to those that mentored me, in many ways my Grandpa Blunt and Grandma Stewart during my earliest years were models of persistent excellence and spiritual depth, respectively, with whom I spent countless hours. With them I always knew I was loved. Joe Stampf, my junior high Sunday school teacher, University of Chicago basketball coach, and gentle giant showed me how to be tough yet kind and to love God deeply. In my adult years, my father in law, Cress Ingle, is the man I wanted to be like and who taught his very clueless son-in-law so much about being a man, a husband, and a follower of Christ. Then, late in life and unexpectedly I had the privilege of working alongside the late Haddon Robinson, an old saint who was tough but tender as a teacher, preacher, pastor, author, and friend. The rest of my mentors came from their books or sermons: C. S. Lewis, Brennan Manning, A. W. Tozer, and Tim Keller.

From Lewis I learned that you don't write a book until it is all you can do. About four years ago, I tried to dampen that prodding sense, but it broke through anyway. Still, I needed confirmation. In the beginning there was B.J. who prayed without ceasing and would not let the idea die. Anne Cregger Patterson who appears here, has her fingerprints all over this in endless conversations and early drafts. It was Anne who led me to Gary Brown who also appears here and who has been such an encouragement when I was stuck. Bruce Fister, my old roomie at the Air Force Academy, also has his story here. Like me he is another unlikely author and "knuckle dragger," who was roped into talking often and reviewing much of the early formless work and as a final reader. All three of these friends joined with my wife to let me know, consistently, they were praying.

As a teacher and sometime writer and speaker, I often find myself surprised that it is Steve Garber, a professor to the nation and now to the world at Regent College, who comes out of my pen or my mouth. Over the last 18 years, his great friendship, collegiality, and personal influence have changed what I think and what I read. He long ago saw the critical role for mentors in shaping young lives, well before I began to think more deeply about all this. Steve, along with Beau Boulter, who has picked me up when I was down and always has an encouraging word, have been twin towers of friendship that surely qualify them as mentors, too.

All those who contributed their stories to this are to be particularly noted as I think these are the heart of the book. For those elders at the gate who have persisted in "a long obedience in the same direction" as mentors to the coming generations, you deserve a "well done" for the wisdom I was fortunate enough to pass on here: Morna Comeau, Kay Hotaling, Rick Woolworth, and Nancy Ziegler along with Gary, Anne, and Bruce.

The other set of stories told about their mentors bookend the elders' stories. I've tried to faithfully pass them on as they were told to me by: Brooks, Steve, Danny, Kate, Al, Adam, David C., Bill, Heather, Doug, Alan, Louise, and Greg. You were so generous to share your lives.

As a layman, I'm loathe to write about the church because I know to some extent how difficult a job that is. Yet, at the end of the day, there is no escaping the fact that great churches nurture great mentors and provide the soil within which intergenerational relationships can bud then flourish. I'm fortunate to have an example I've lived within for nearly ten years—Restoration Anglican Church in Arlington, Virginia. I owe a huge debt to my pastor, David Hanke, and to my good friend and our Youth Director, Isaiah Brooms, for sharing their stories, wisdom, and teaching. It was important that people see all this is not just theory but incarnated fact. I'd also be remiss not to include the guys from my men's small group that meets at the ungodly hour of 6:30 am to share our lives and to mentor each other. You have encouraged and prayed for this project, and in ways I am too blind to see helped shape it. I hope we can continue on and spread what we have to other guys of all ages.

In keeping with what I've written, it is hard to separate the benefits I have received in being a father, grandfather, and older friend to so many younger people whether singles or couples, students or those deep in the "valley of the diapers." I have been taught in so many ways by those coming after me who have been patient with my "lectures," and I pray each of you will turn around to those coming behind you for you will be blessed as I have been. A special thanks for patience and tolerating my long-windedness to our daughter, Robin Luckenbaugh and her husband Dean (also my boss); Matt Blunt and his wife Sheryl; and our grandchildren, Rachel, Joshua, and Jake Luckenbaugh and Carissa and Audrey Blunt. How bare would be our lives without you.

Then, somehow, Mike Parker, WordCrafts Press founder and publisher came alongside and helped steer me through the labyrinth. His wisdom and encouragement have meant so much and have helped buff something that had more roughness than I knew. Thanks my friend.

Finally, the greatest influence on this work and on my life has been my Father, my Lord and Savior, and the Paraclete, the One who came alongside to inspire, guide, and empower this project; He chased me down when I wandered so that I could share the lessons of wisdom born out of much failure. Only You know how often I prayed when this seemed a jumble and only You deserve all the glory. Soli Deo Gloria.

About the Author

Ray Blunt is an elder at the gate who for the last thirty years describes his primary focus as helping to grow the next generation of servant leaders. Today he teaches high school juniors and seniors philosophy, sociology, and theology at Ad Fontes Academy, a classical Christian school in Centreville, Virginia, where he has taught four of his grandchildren. Before then he was an Associate Professor in Leadership at Gordon Conwell Theological Seminary, teaching in a DMin program and also consulted on leadership development and organizational culture to dozens of organizations. Before then he served in public service as a senior leader whose focus was strategic planning, human capital, and organizational effectiveness. Long ago, he was in one of the first classes to graduate from the U.S. Air Force Academy in 1964 and went on to achieve master's degrees in comparative economics and theology.

He has written extensively on leadership, organizational culture, and character. His first book was *Crossed Lives, Crossed Purposes: Why Thomas Jefferson Failed and William Wilberforce Persisted in Leading an End to Slavery,* (Eugene, Oregon: Wipf & Stock Publishers, 2012) and contributed a chapter to The Jossey-Bass Reader on Non Profit and Public Leadership, James L. Perry, ed., "How Leaders Are Grown," (San Francisco: Jossey-Bass, 2010).

He and his wife, B.J., have been married for over 50 years and attend Restoration Anglican Church where they have mentored more than 20 young couples before and after marriage. He sees his role in this third third of life as continuing to teach, to mentor younger men and women in their emerging adult years, and to speak to anyone who will listen, including grandchildren of course. Hiking, kayaking and biking give him not only waning fitness but sanity and time to be alone with God and enjoy his marvelous creation.

ALSO AVAILABLE FROM

WordCrafts Press

A Revelation of Love
    by Jill Grossman

Confounding the Wise
    by Dan Kulp

Pondering(s)
    by Wayne Berry

Ditch the Drama
    by Ginny Priz

Morning Mist: Stories from the Water's Edge
    by Barbie Loflin

Youth Ministry is Easy! and 9 other lies
    by Aaron Shaver

Illuminations
    by Paula K. Parker & Tracy Sugg

www.wordcrafts.net

CPSIA information can be obtained
at www.ICGtesting.com
Printed in the USA
LVHW04s0739091018
592838LV00008B/19/P